OUTSIDE THE LINES

(Memoirs Of A Naughty Boy #2)

OUTSIDE THE LINES

Nothing is as you perceive
Look beyond the beyond
Where the wind whips the sea
Unicorns roam
Shadows run free
There you may find the answers you seek
I can only guide you
You alone will know the truth once found
Run with the wolves
Travel when the moon shines full
Go and change the stars
Barukh Salaam
(Gifted to Manassah Bin Barukh)

Memoirs Of A Naughty Boy #2

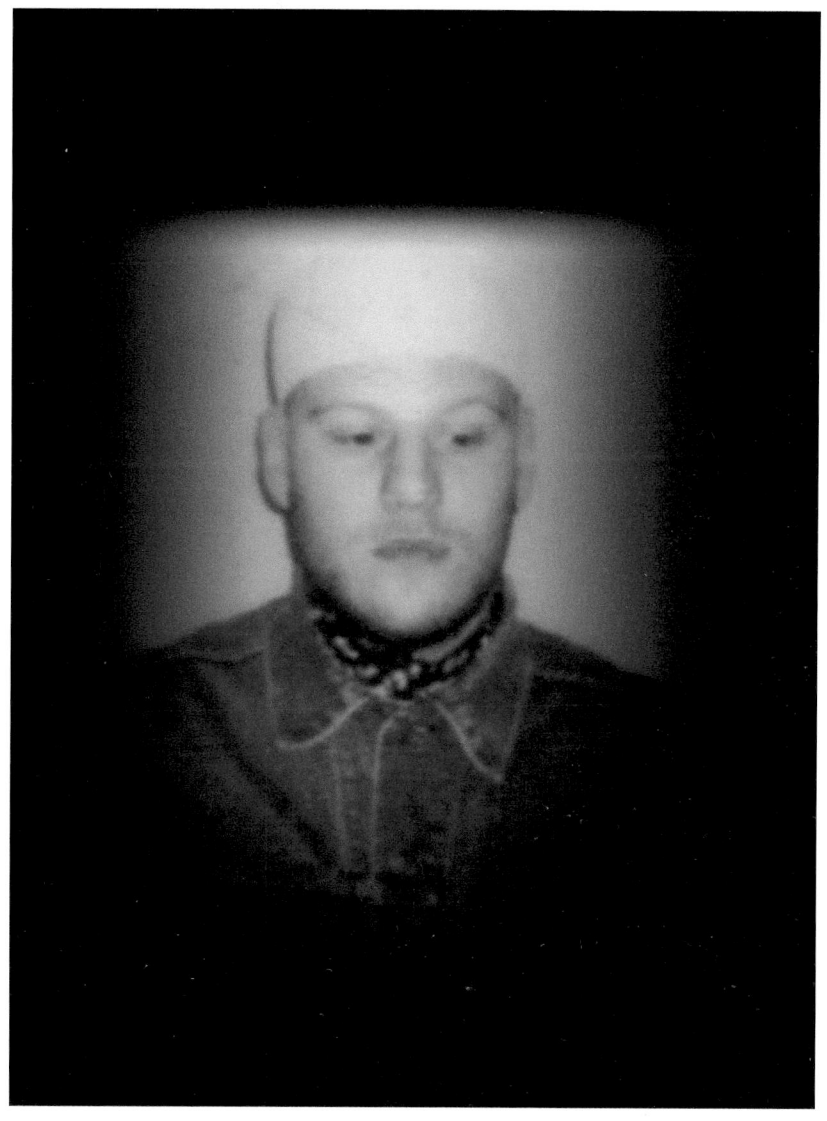

1993 - 'Best Of British Men'

OUTSIDE THE LINES

Writing gives one an opportunity to show who one really is - displaying a vulnerability that cannot be revealed in the real world…

I write my truth as I choose to tell it
This is who I am - judge me as you wish
Your perception of me is not my business
I am a product of the time that I evolved in.
The product became the producer…

My writing is not grammatically correct - I did not intend it to be. What you are reading is a document written in my voice. This is how I think - how I talk - how I articulate: often contradictory…

2013 - Philosophising - Jon & Me - V&A - Shot By Iain Akal

Jon Daniel

I dedicate this second book to the memory of a man who motivated me upon my journey to become a writer. When I was in doubt he engaged me with a creative courage that would facilitate me to fulfil my potential as a storyteller.

He gifted me books, explained the intricacies of Adobe and was always at the end of the phone when I was in need of level advice. We spent many long afternoons exchanging creative concepts - however, it would be he that always followed through to make the phone call or send the email to connect with the correct person.

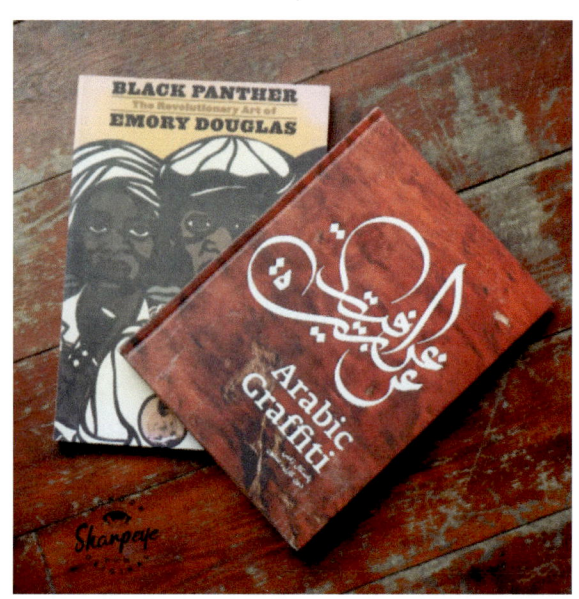

Gifts From Jon

When we first met I encouraged him to explore further as a creative - I felt he was not accomplishing his innovative capacity - his talents marginalised.

I finished my first book and he named it 'This Was Not Part Of The Masterplan' - too undisguised for my esoteric taste: yet perfect.

Jon Daniel believed in me more than I believed in myself…

Thank you for this lovely dedication to Jon; I know that he would be so honoured to be spoken of this way because your opinion meant a lot to him and you say what you mean, honestly. He would also have played down his input, saying that he only gave you a slight nudge. He got so much out of your friendship and would always come home buzzing after spending time with you… (Jane Daniel)

Jon and his wife Jane

Barrie K. Sharpe - Hustler Of Inspiration

The Name, I had known for years, initially through his Acid Jazz breakthrough track, Masterplan. But I would not come to know The Man until many years later. Unlike many of his followers who were either Rare Groove, Wag Club or Duffer fanatics, I didn't really take notice of Barrie until he started his Sharpeye label in West Soho in the 90s.

It's difficult to convey the impact that his Sharpeye store had on me, but just like the ultra-modernist utilitarian clothes hanging off the metal rails on butcher's meat hooks, I was utterly hooked. Like so much of Barrie's work, it touched me on several levels: aesthetically, intellectually, emotionally, culturally and ideologically.

However, I still did not get to meet Barrie in person until much later, around 2007.

As a newer friend of Barrie, I think I naturally have a different perspective from those who have known him since his heyday. He's a cat who wears many hats; a pioneer, a dancer, a club DJ, a bandleader, a producer; a fashion designer, an entrepreneur, a loyal friend: a devoted father. This much is already well known.

OUTSIDE THE LINES

But in the relatively short time I've known him, I've also seen him emerge as an artist, a writer, a photographer, a filmmaker and a freedom fighter. All pulled off with the steadfast, uncompromising style and attitude that is his trademark.

I've also noticed that Barrie is like many of his peers, who often struggle with legitimising their achievements, because at the time they were breaking new ground by doing things that had either never been done or were not condoned by the industry or the Establishment; turning their passions into professions and redefining underground youth culture in the process.

As someone who has worked as a creative professional in the advertising and design industry for over 25 years, Barrie is one of the most consummate creatives I have ever met. He lives his life to his own design and creates beautiful pieces to suit every aspect of it. From the clothes he wears, to the bikes he rides, to the music he plays, to the home that he has created; a living museum to his life, style and attitude, that leaves me with nothing but deep admiration.

As a friend, Barrie is a constant source of inspiration and encouragement to me to live my own life on my own terms. In return, I try to help him in any way I can to gain the recognition his extraordinary talent deserves and to take his rightful place as one of the most culturally influential people of our times.

His story is a testament to that fact... (The words of Jon Daniel - the original 'Afro Supa Hero')

Reading this piece again I realise Jon is still a great inspiration and his words still as motivating. Unfortunately he is no longer a phone call away - a vacant in space in my creative soul…

Memoirs Of A Naughty Boy #2

From The Original Afro Supa Hero Series Created By Jon Daniel -
Adapted For Book Cover

OUTSIDE THE LINES

Preface
At no time in my life did I ever expect to be writing a book - my only regret is that my father did not live to read it.

This book was no easy task - I lost two people who were paramount to me finishing my first book. One being Jon - the other was the only person that I ever trusted to show me the way.

Before writing the previous book I had never written a story. Before mastering a computer I was unable to write. Since my first book in many ways my writing and articulation have greatly improved - I am freer with what I am willing to reveal and comfortably more descriptive.

Rarely does the way one makes a living or one's job define one: what I do for a living - 'my job' - does define me - it is who I am - my lifestyle - my passion.

It may seem that I perform a variety of creative tasks yet for me the creative process is all one and the same. Many perceive me as some kind of artist - I am actually a problem solver. I look at the project in hand and figure out the simplest way to achieve the preferred solution - continuing until accomplishing the desired result - failure not an option.

Like many creatives I am always expecting people to find out that I am bluffing and actually have absolutely no idea of what I am doing - yet I keep on doing.

I am always expecting to run out of new ideas - but each and every morning I awake with fresh challenges. My constant question to myself is always - 'how did I get here'…?

The Twisted Mind Of The Aquarian Creative
2020 - (This is where I am at)
Before joining Facebook I did/could not write and cared very little about it.
Upon seeing political - racist - bigoted - misogynistic - homophobic FB posts:
I began to question
I started to argue
I started to debate
I started to fuck people right off

OUTSIDE THE LINES

More importantly I realised that I could succinctly, articulately, using no extra words take people to the cleaners: I found this empowering.
From there I went on to write a book
Turned down by all publishers
Crowd-funded
Self-published
Now in the British Library, university libraries and many college libraries.

Since mastering the computer keyboard I have recently taught myself the skills of penmanship. I perceive the pen may not be as mighty as the sword - yet I reckon it could do some serious damage…

Book 2
Without realising it I began writing a second book but I stopped about two years ago due to being overawed by someone, whom I perceive to be more intelligent, telling me that my words were not as evocative as I thought they were. I started to question everything that I wrote. Normally I would have carried on regardless, I am used to criticism, yet at the time I was recovering from a mental health issue hence unsure of myself. It transpired that some months earlier I had contracted a urinary tract infection which had caused mild dementia. No one had noticed that I had been acting a little bit odd for some time. I only found out due to a motorbike accident that caused me some kidney damage - the recovery period was longer than I had realised.

All of my life I have done my own thing - my way:
Hustled
Trusted my instinct
Relied upon very few
Played my own game

Asked a lot of questions
Solved my own problems
Came up with my own solutions
Unless asked for, took little advice
Generally fell in the right direction

Overall I have done okay, I've achieved many things, yet still occasionally fail. My first failure being school; although I was able to get an education I struggled academically - the reason came to light later in life.

Dyslexia does not mean that one is 'stupid, thick, bone idle, lazy or a fucking moron' - it just means that one is different. It is not a disease/affliction/disability - it is a gift. One who is dyslexic is often super creative, smart and able to see situations from an alternative logical perspective - a lateral thinker. The upside for me - I have a semi-photographic memory and a Sharpe-eye for detail. I am perceptive, creative and as Sharpe as a weasel. The downside - I cannot write properly with a pen and have extreme difficulty in putting my letters in the correct order - which has led to OCD. Creatively I owe it all to LSD, Sesame Street and hustling...

Who I Am
I have only ever had one real job - I naturally relied upon my instinct and worked my way through things.

I am unsure how I got here - what I do know is that if you can do it I can do it.

What people often fail to realise is that I only know what they know - I did not create anything new - I merely changed what I saw - I am still trying to figure

OUTSIDE THE LINES

things out.

Over the years the people that have tried to put the pieces of my puzzle in the correct position have done me a disservice: the pieces are displaced for good reason.

I listen
I like to write
I study people
I have few friends
I look at everything
I do not do small talk
I do my best thinking alone
I spend much time on my own
I am uncomfortable in a crowd
My inner monologue never stops
I collaborate with very few people
If I am not being creative I get bored
I shut down after too much socialising
I concentrate on things that matter to me
In a flamboyant fashion I am an introvert
I pay attention to minor details that others miss
I prefer writing my thoughts than speaking them
I alternate between being social and being solitary

Upon my journey I have left a 'vast legacy'. People treat me with much respect, indeed many hero worship - I cannot see why and struggle to accept. I feel superficial - fooling the public - always that I am a charlatan expecting to be found out or possibly run out of the fresh ideas that forever keep me present. I am often placed upon an undeserved pedestal - many would like to see me fall -

some attempt to push me off.

Usually I crave anonymity: shunning praise - love - sympathy - affection. On the other hand I seek recognition.

I am not a leader
I am not a radical
I am not a team player
I am not a revolutionary
I am not a public speaker

However:
I will question
I will speak my mind
I will exchange views
I will not be dictated to
I will not accept injustice
I will not tolerate ignorance

Saying that:
I do attend protests
I am one of the people
I do support insurrection
I am willing to bleed for what I believe

Do not underestimate the power of the word - if you change the mind of one you may change the future - if you change the minds of many you may shape the future.

I prefer my words to be balanced within an unbalanced world…

OUTSIDE THE LINES

Introduction
I realised from a young age that there was another way that I could persevere in the world other than that what was bestowed upon or expected of me. There were no limitations - no boundaries - mediocrity was not ever an option.

Although of immigrant stock I descend from the Dickensian Dodger
Hustle as the Costermonger once did on the same East End streets
I too wanted and deserved more - "MORE!"
A fly pitcher - "Ave it up"
Eyes peeled working on the Run-Out
"I'll pay you little - nick all you can"
"If I catch you I'll break your fuckin' 'ands"
The stinking funkum we punted on Oxford Street
The Jekyll perfume sold for much more than it's worth
The profit spunked on the geegees
"Sorry son - I'll pay ya t'mora"
My journey here was through the London streets
I just kept falling uphill.

I guess the reason that I was so quiet in my younger days was due to my fast East End accent - running one word into the next: no beginning - no end - no full stop - no rest - no time to breathe. No one knew what the hell I was going on about. The more I wanted to tell my story and the more excited I got the less I was understood.

I am telling this story as I wish to remember it. My dates and facts are out of sequence - my tale is based upon memory and hearsay thus cannot guarantee all to be true.

I designed the clothes

Memoirs Of A Naughty Boy #2

1965

OUTSIDE THE LINES

Ran the club
Played the records
Was in the band
Made the music
All of which created the scene that changed youth culture worldwide.
I just kept falling upwards.

Right place - right time: I invented nothing - I merely re-sculptured to my personal taste. I have my own style ideology - my game my rules.

It has never been my intention to 'rock the boat' - I have always tried to capsize the ship.

My attitude defined a special moment in time…

Me
This is a factual non-emotional account of 'my facts'.

As a child I was diagnosed as 'stupid' - fortunately I had other ideas.

Although I usually had the support of my father constantly being rejected has left its scars yet given me the skills to go it alone, regardless of the rejection.

As a creative I often struggle with normality. I am impulsive and in one way or another have to express what I feel - although not always through language nor written word. If I get a notion to do something I have to do it - I have to investigate - I have to take on the challenge: even take a gamble. Never perturbed by risks, I weigh up the negatives (never the positives) and proceed regardless of the possibility of failure. Fortunately, creatively I do not remember any failures - I merely continue until I succeed.

My mind is transient - always open to change at any given moment. I welcome new information, I am willing to listen and learn: I have no issue in changing horses mid-race.

However, I am not as confident as I may portray. I always think that I need advice - never sure if I have got things right - perhaps seeking approval. In many ways I am un-harmonious when alone. As I am often alone I have to endeavour through my disabilities and insecurities. I recognise my inabilities and when I can I am not ashamed to ask for help. I have no plans: I do not consider myself a forward thinker - I merely function upon a spur of the moment whim - constantly falling uphill.

In the past I have had help - that period was creatively my happiest and most consistently productive - knowing that I had the approval and support of another. Unfortunately, as a creative I possibly gave much less in return - caught up in my own expression: not knowing how to give. I am reclusive and although I do need others I am often dismissive of people.

I put myself into life and life happened around me - navigating through the turbulence not knowing in which direction I was travelling. Without support I struggled with day-to-day normality yet I create a solid foundation out of shifting sands…

How I Feel
Due to the following I struggle to accept sympathy or praise: both makes me uncomfortable. I am not even sure if I wish to be loved, cared for or nurtured - I have not learnt how: way out of my comfort zone.

OUTSIDE THE LINES

1961 - 'Uncle Tom's Cabin' - Southend

For my whole life I have felt rejected - having to fight every step of the way with no support - no one told me that I was good at anything - I had to devise my own coping mechanisms. Even now with all my achievements I struggle to value my own worth or believe in myself - my accomplishments. I am always waiting for people to find out that I am bluffing. I merely do what feels right for me: I tend to fall upwardly.

My mother rejected me - never held or hugged me - no words of encouragement. I felt unloved and unlovable. She was ill: I have never blamed her - it was not her fault.

My father was a man that could cope with anything - unfortunately on his own he could not cope with my sister and me. Due to our childhood experiences I feel that my sister's damage is far greater than mine. It was the 1960s, a time when children were confiscated from single mothers - this was not a time when fathers brought up or cared for their children alone. Again I do not blame him - it was the period that we lived in.

My father was distant and my mother did not always know who I was.

From a young age I played alone in my fantasy world - due to my transient upbringing I had few friends. At school I was never picked for anything. Although I was a fair player I never made the football team - in fact all that did was put me off football. I could run, jump and throw but was always passed by for the athletics team - no one noticed me - I gave up.

I struggled to read and write - indeed I struggled to comprehend most things at school - I was labelled an 'idiot'. No - I was something unheard of back then: I was fucking dyslexic. I would not and did not accept that I was an idiot: because I was not. This is where my father came into-his-own: he too would not accept that I was an idiot.

Although it was hard and I hated his tuition, he taught me to read and almost write: he taught me many things. When trying to help my own son with his homework in his eyes I saw the same stress and confusion that I experienced - I was no academic teacher hence I stopped trying to be one.

OUTSIDE THE LINES

I did make a strong bond with Marcia May but she too was damaged and her fondness for me quite twisted. Eventually she would leave me - again no blame - she took her own life.

My greatest joy was the discovery of music and dancing: my saviour - I fitted in. I frequented places that were predominantly black; this was where I felt most comfortable and accepted. It was like I had a secret parallel life - I had my white Jewish friends and my black friends - rarely did my two worlds eclipse.

I danced - wore nice clothes - dated girls - eventually discovering LSD The girl thing was strange; I had no idea how to communicate with them - communicate with anyone for that matter. I could dance - girls liked boys who could dance - it meant that they were apparently 'a good fuck'.

This was how I stumbled along: clubs - dancing - girls - dance classes - ballet - LSD. I enjoyed my life, I was comfortable in this world. I did not need to talk, smile nor pretend to be friendly - I was left alone to do my thing. I only ever had the one job and that just for a few months: I had neither skills nor work ethic. I did crap at school, leaving with no qualifications - yet I did have an education: thanks to my dad I went to a Grammar school. Later he secured me a place at St Martin's School of Art by sending them my art: record sleeves that I had designed in Magic Marker. My dad bought me Magic Markers so I drew. I did not go to St. Martin's - I did not have the confidence: besides they would have found out that I was bluffing.

Eventually I became a DJ at the trendiest nightclub in the world - through this I was at the forefront of a new musical movement. I was one of the four that created the world's trendiest fashion label - changing the face of world fashion (we shook it all up). I was one of the two DJs and creators of an iconic underground nightclub that changed the whole underground club scene. I was

Memoirs Of A Naughty Boy #2

*Magic Marker Copy
Of The Record Sleeve
'The World Is A Ghetto'
By War*

in the band that became the three bands that forefronted a whole new music style. None of these things were planned - I would never have dreamt of rising so far above my station. I was bluffing. I became a single father and gave it all up to care for my son.

Bored with the lack of creativity I created a new iconic fashion label for the Japanese market: eventually having five London stores. I did so much, with much success - still I knew that I was bluffing.

In later years I found one person that I thought believed in and supported me - I was wrong. I was on my own in my own private world of creative mayhem. I build bicycles and motorbikes - take photos - make films - write/record/produce music - design/produce clothing: I do stuff - so much stuff. I am now a successful writer - (to reiterate) I even have my book in the British Library - how the fuck did I become a writer? How did I get here? I saw none of this coming. Still I feel like I am that kid - bluffing.

OUTSIDE THE LINES

Right now I have a cult fashion label - a cult music following - a very credible underground club night - a vast following on social media: I keep it moving.

Anything I share on social media is not the truth: merely my perception.

Even in my subsequent years I am still current - still present. So when am I going to be caught out? When will all see that I am actually bluffing?

My secret is to flounder near the top - never peaking: once one peaks the only way is down.

"Never put yourself in a position that allows others to control your life" - Raul Bin Benjamin (Ronald Harvey Sharpe) - my father…

My Parents
Why is my mother on the floor screaming - arms strapped to her sides - buckled securely in a harsh dirty white jacket?
What has she done wrong?
Why are they not listening to her?
Why does no one care?
Why won't they let her go?
'WHY ~ WHY ~ WHY'!
(Restriction - my greatest fear).

They dragged her away to be shocked - she would forget me again - she always forgot me once they gave her shock treatment.

September 2019 - I visited Goodmayes Hospital to take some photos. I had to climb over the fence because the hospital has been closed for many years.

Memoirs Of A Naughty Boy #2

Goodmayes Mental Health Institution - Where My Mother Resided For Half Of My Pre-Teens Life

Two security guards questioned me as to my presence on the hospital grounds. I explained that my mum had once lived and indeed died there. They were sympathetic and let me take some photos.

One engaged me in conversation. "There is actually a horror movie being shot in there at the moment - it's a scary place at night: a real horror show."
I replied - "I know."

Often my mother would still be serving Sunday's cold and dry roasted leg of lamb and baked potatoes on a Thursday. On two occasions I found maggots in the meat: it was not that we were poor - it was simply that my mum had lost her connection with reality.

OUTSIDE THE LINES

To suggest that her cooking was mediocre would be a compliment - it was bland and the portions small: she may have been the worst cook in the entire world. The long-term effect upon me is that even if I am full I will eat all that is put in front of me and I continue eating until every morsel is consumed. I also eat very fast - once I start I will not stop until my plate is empty: I perceive that this aspect of my behaviour is the consequence of living in children's homes or foster care (children would steal other children's food). I like to eat socially but I am always finished before anyone else; except maybe my son, he eats just as fast as me - I guess that is my fault.

On the upside - my mother made great chips, brilliant roast potatoes and the best cheesecake in the world.

Although the relationship with my father was turbulent it is now coming to pass that many of my perceptions are based upon his views. At 15 years old he gave me Malcolm X's biography. He explained why he thought Martin Luther King and Gandhi were tools of government to appease the masses. "By preaching peace and not revolution they suppressed their own people." When I played the record 'Free Nelson Mandela' my father talked of Steve Biko.

After watching the biopic movie 'Selma' my personal views changed - I realised that it was MLK's intension to incite extreme violence in others.

My father's quest for knowledge was limited to libraries and reading - he did not have the immediate information at his fingertips - he could not cross reference worldwide information in a matter of minutes: he studied book-by-book.

I wonder what his views would have been had he the power of the World Wide Web?

Memoirs Of A Naughty Boy #2

1942 - Mum - 10 Years Old - & Grandpa Sid

OUTSIDE THE LINES

His thoughts on Colonel Gaddafi?
Saddam Hussein?
The Western deconstruction of the Middle East?
The allegiance between Israel - Egypt - Saudi?
Extreme right-wing militants flying the Israeli flag?

He had strong views on the American Civil Rights Movement - how would he feel about the present situation and the impression that we are seemly losing ground instead of progressing? Would his views have differed had he been able to access the Internet?

We now have the privilege of watching and reading the daily news and then within seconds we can cross-reference with unlimited sources. We may not be fed the truth yet we have the power and knowledge to decipher for ourselves and create our own perceptions.

As my father he was not a great role model and did little to prepare me for fatherhood - he did not know how.

As a man he taught me much:
He taught me survival
To know who I am
To trust no man's word
To stand up for my beliefs
To be self-sufficient
To be compassionate
To help others in need
Reliability (I am a man of my word)
Trustworthiness
To act as an individual (when others turn right - do not be afraid to go left)

1955 - Mr & Mrs Sharpe

Honesty (except in matters of business finance)
To know when to stand and fight and when to stand down
Never to back down if I perceive that I am right
To know when I am wrong
To be transient of mind
Not to say too much (people only know what you tell them)
Not to be intimidated by a posh accent (people pretend to be something that they are not)

OUTSIDE THE LINES

Never look down upon another
Treat people with respect (I am not more important)
Stand up to bullies
To question (the man who seeks knowledge is already wise)
Most importantly - he taught me to think.

On the other hand - I once experienced a different side to my usually level-headed father. He saw my sister in the car of her black boyfriend (a drummer in a reggae band) - they were kissing. He went outside, ordered her into the house, was abusive to the boyfriend and did not hesitate to use the 'N' word when later berating her. This was a most stressful eye-opener for me: contradictory to the logic that my father always spoke and alien to my upbringing. It changed my view of my father forever. My sister never forgave him.

There was also the moment when my parents first saw my son.
My mum commented. "He's not that dark."
This had obviously been a previous point of discussion between them.
I replied defiantly. "Don't worry - he'll get darker as he gets older."

I have never mourned the death of my father nor my mother - I don't know how…

Late 1960s
A random memory (this only just came to me). It was pouring with rain so I went home around 7pm to watch the television. Unfortunately my dad was watching adult stuff - boring old men talking. He was engrossed in an interview with some old geezer with an uncomfortably strange posh accent on the David Frost Show.

The old geezer was a man named Oswald Mosley talking about men in black shirts - he had an odd way of pronouncing his words. Due to my dad's agitation it was memorable. He disappeared for a minute or two, rummaging around the house and returning with a hammer which he then proceeded to put through the television screen. Expressing - "Fascist piece of shit…!"

Who Was My Father…?
1963-67 - I always had a rough idea of what my father was about and kind of had a handle on his history.

His father, a Palestinian refugee, refused to pay extortion money to local street gangsters - for his refusal he was brutally assaulted: he died after suffering a massive heart attack. Apparently my father's retribution for this act was bloody and final.

He once mentioned that just after my birth he spent a few months in Israel. He was working with El Al (the Israeli airline) while Mossad was bringing in a captured Nazi war criminal. My father was tasked with keeping the transportation drama out of the press and the public eye: I am sure a much easier feat back then than it would be today. With modern research facilities it took me less than a minute to figure out that the war criminal he referred to was Adolf Eichmann. My father - Israel - Mossad - El Al - a strange combination considering his political stance - it does not add up. However, it was one of the few stories that he relayed to me himself so possibly one that is more than likely true.

The following has been on my mind for quite a while - today is the day to write it.

OUTSIDE THE LINES

Circa 1963, and for a few years following, my father would pack the whole family and Julie into his latest car (he always had a brand spanking new car) and take us on a journey across Europe into the Eastern Bloc. A ferry to Boulogne or Ostend and a long drive through Italy - Spain - Germany - Norway - Sweden - Switzerland - Belgium - Greece - Turkey - Yugoslavia - Romania - Czechoslovakia - Bulgaria - Hungary: all the way to the Black Sea. I am not sure of the correct order but these were the countries that we visited - I still have a huge box full of the various coins as a memento.

Julie - who the hell was Julie? I only recently discovered her name during an email exchange with my sister (who resides in Canada). I had to confirm that we did actually go on these epic car trips: she confirmed that we did. I guess Julie was in her 20s. To my recollection a tall - slim - pretty - olive skinned - short brown haired - foreign accented woman: that is all I or my sister know. Oh yes, she was a strong swimmer: I used to cling onto the back of her broad shoulders while she swam in the sea. I have no more information.

I have very few memories of these journeys, but the ones I do have are quite vivid. I remember my dad and Julie going off with men in smart suits and big cars and not coming back for the whole day or a couple of days - while my mum, sister and I stayed behind in the various hotels.

We often stayed in establishments that had not been used for decades. Dusty and full of cobwebs with brown running tap water: the whole thing was like a fuckin' fairy-tale. I now realise that we were in small Eastern European villages. I remember driving through Romania on dirt roads and workers coming out of the fields to look at the car as if it was their first time seeing such a vehicle. Then the overseers with long whips telling us to move on and ordering the workers back into the fields.

1973

We passed a police checkpoint on the Carpathian Mountains at dusk and entered onto a bridge, by the time we reached the other end of the bridge the gates were firmly closed. We attempted to go back only to find that the gates we entered through were now also shut and locked. We had to spend the night sleeping in the car on the bridge. We were in Transylvania which of course had no significance to me at the time.

Hot sun - long empty beaches - the warm Black Sea. I ran into the waves after my dad - then a haze - I was engulfed in misty salty bottomless water. I had stepped off a sandbar into the deep abyss - I did not know it but I was drowning. I struggled - twisted - spluttered yet could not catch my breath: then peace - back in the womb. It seemed like forever before huge strong hands grabbed me. I came back to reality on the shoulders of a stranger who spoke words that I had never heard before: he was Turkish.

OUTSIDE THE LINES

Whilst reminiscing I have completely digressed from the point of this piece.

When I told my schoolteacher of my summer travels, in front of the class she accused me of lying (for reasons I now understand) and invited my dad to the school for 'a word'.

"Barrie has described detailed journeys into the Eastern Bloc, we are concerned regarding these huge lies he tells."

My dad was silent for quite a while. "We did indeed travel to the countries that he has described, yet what concerns me is you calling my son a liar in front of the entire class. I am not asking, I am telling you to publicly apologise!"

I told my girlfriend - knowledgeable in everything - of these travels. She immediately contested. "How could you have gone to these places in the early 60s? There were stringent travel restrictions imposed upon entering Eastern Europe". She went on to explain that visas would have needed to be obtained to cross each of the separate borders and these were only available to some diplomats. Even diplomats were not allowed to cross the borders by car.

It has been suggested that my father was a spy an arms dealer - a diplomat - blackmailed by the authorities to do some clandestine deed; all of which I believe to be untrue...

The Missing Walnuts
1964 (4 years old) - I was living in Harold Wood Hall children's home at Gallows Corner. Too young for school - hence in the daytime I was left to my own devices. Usually I wandered in the surrounding cow fields looking for mischief. On one occasion I took my teddy bear into the huge kitchen and proceeded

to wash it in one of the large sinks using a scrubbing brush and lashings of washing up liquid: the mess I left was catastrophic. Without much effort matron discovered me - I had left a long water trail all the way to the upstairs boys communal bathroom where I was hanging my bear up to dry. I was punished severely.

My sister said that she remembered Matron (Mrs Golightly) as a 'complete bitch'.

It was late summer - the days were shorter, the mornings breezy and the sun not so warming. I was sitting on the outside steps of the huge kitchen where stood a monumental walnut tree. I rarely got a look in on the walnuts as all the bigger kids were in there first, or they would simply just take mine. Now was my chance.

There was an array of fresh walnuts on the ground but I preferred to climb the thick trunk of the tree and shake the walnuts free from the branches simply for the hell of it. I was always looking for adventure: I was a risk taker and liked an element of danger.

I gathered up a large brown paper bag full (the kind that was used at the greengrocers for fruit and veg). Of course I cracked open and ate as many as I had saved; they made my mouth sore but that did not discourage me. I was the emperor of the walnut tree.

What was I going to do with my veritable treasure? I had already scoffed myself to the point of near sickness; I would have to stash them until a later date. I decided to hide them in a top cubby of the pea green pigeonholes that entirely covered one of the walls of the playroom. It was quite a feat to climb, at least fourteen feet high: to a 4-year-old - Mount Everest.

OUTSIDE THE LINES

I climbed up the left side, stepping onto the first shelf then dragging myself up to the second. I continued up via this method: it was strenuous but I was determined. One shelf at a time I climbed. I was getting tired and my arms were aching: two more to go. Once I reached my destination there was a dilemma - I wanted to stash my treasure in the middle pigeonhole. I shimmied along until I was satisfied with my chosen location. The shelves were deep so I had to climb inside to place the walnuts in the corner. Climbing down was a much simpler task - with a big leap before I reached the bottom: which hurt my knees.

The snow was falling - it was nearly Christmas and my dad was coming to take me home (I cried writing that). The kids were at the window watching the snowflakes falling. The fields were completely white and we were not allowed out to play. My brain kicked in: 'my walnuts! - I must get my walnuts'. Most of the kids were in the lounge - only a few of the younger children were playing in the playroom. I repeated my previous upward journey with ease. I shimmied along and climbed into the cubby but it was empty - they were gone! I cried for a minute or two and then climbed back down slowly. I joined the rest of the kids at the window in the lounge and waited for my dad…

Nothing Of The Sort/Salt
1964 - Another story set in Harold Wood Hall children's home.

Mr Doyle was as always very cross and he usually carried a swishy flexible cane. It was daybreak we were all ordered out of bed: the bright morning sunlight burned my eyes.

"Which one of you made that loud racket last night - or was it all of you?" He demanded of the eldest Boyle brother.
The eldest Boyle brother pointed at me.

Harold Wood Hall - Shot By Roger Atkinson

"Who was it?" He asked one of the Boyle twins.
The Boyle twin pointed at me.
"Who was it?" He asked the other Boyle twin.
The other Boyle twin pointed at me.
"Was it you Sharpe?"
"No sir - it was them."
"Are you bloody stupid boy? I asked if it was you: I didn't ask you whom it was!"
"But sir, you did ask."
"I asked nothing of the sort!"
I laughed.
"What are laughing at boy?"
"You said nothing of the salt."
I laughed again.

OUTSIDE THE LINES

"I said nothing of the sort!"
Not understanding the severity of my situation I continued laughing.
"Put out both hands boy."
"No!"

I turned to run - I was not going to allow him to beat me with his cane again. The Boyle brothers prevented my escape - all three wrestled me to the floor of the small stark dormitory. "Get out of the way boys, Sharpe is going to get the beating of his life."

Still on the floor I tried to get away but it was futile, my path was blocked - I was trapped. "Right you cocky little bastard, you have had this coming for a while." He swished the whistling cane through the air striking me on the thigh; I screamed - then the buttocks - then the back - then the upper arm. He kept on thrashing me while the Boyles looked on and laughed.

I did not cry, I never cried in front of my punisher, although tears streamed down my face.

"Got something to say now boy?"
"You fucking cunt!"

He beat me until I was unconscious and then locked me in one of the huge floor to ceiling cupboards that were fitted in all the dormitories - all were painted with thick pea green paint.

I should have told my dad, but I knew my dad would have killed him and gone to prison…

Inside The Lines
1966 - As was often the case my mum was in hospital. My sister and I were sent to stay with the family of a boy who went to my school. I know it was 1966 because for compensation I had been given the choice of having a World Cup Willie toy (the 1966 world cup mascot) or a Dalek - I went for the Dalek.

The Silvermans were a strange Jewish family. David was the year above me at school, Jeremy was younger and their sister Susan was in the same class as my sister. I don't really remember Mrs Silverman very well but I know Mr Silverman was estranged and lived elsewhere. I remember going to see him selling toys in an auction: I am sure that his hands were adorned with Sooty and Sweep glove puppets.

Whilst at the Silvermans I got quite ill. As was usual at the time Mrs Silverman acquired for me - from Dr Compton-Smith (my regular GP - a monocled man) - some kaolin and morphine. I liked it; it brought on drowsiness that led to a deep sleep and dreams. Mrs Silverman was getting worried, I had been ill for quite a while so she called my dad to get him to come and see for himself. He turned up early one morning to discuss my condition. We sat around the kitchen table whilst Mrs Silverman explained the situation.

The whole time they were chatting my dad was staring at the bottle of kaolin and morphine. The kaolin had settled and had separated from the morphine.

"You see that clear liquid at the top of the bottle - that is morphine. Morphine is like heroin. You do not give children heroin!"
She retorted. "But it was prescribed by Dr Compton-Smith."
He was annoyed. "I don't care who prescribed it. It is morphine, addictive and potentially lethal for a 6-year-old child you stupid cow."

OUTSIDE THE LINES

"Barrie - get your coat on!" I never went back there.

I was actually quite weak and seriously ill. We drove to King George Hospital; which at the time was in Newbury Park. Back then if you were ill you could go straight to the Casualty Department and be seen by a doctor within 10 minutes: I should know - as a kid I spent much time in Casualty.

I was diagnosed with the mumps and was immediately admitted into a tiny single room - I am not sure whether I was quarantined or not - anyway I was stuck on my own with absolutely nothing to do.

My dad would regularly visit - he brought me a Batman colouring book and wax crayons, insisting that I was only allowed to do the colouring in when he was there. He was trying to teach me to colour inside the lines. Of course once he left I continued colouring: I did not have a white crayon so I used yellow for the faces. I never quite learned to colour inside the lines (plus - although it was not recognised until I was 16 - I was colour-blind).

Hospitals used to be run by matrons and ward sisters, supported by nurses. All ran as clockwork - patients were seen quickly, hospital beds available and the quality of care was outstanding. After an operation patients stayed in the wards until they had recouped.

I perceive that the demise of the modern NHS is the fault of the executive governing bodies - non-medical professionals who run it as a business with no actual consideration for healthcare. A complete and utter mess...

Genie And Michael

1969 - In my pre-teens I felt of little worth - although compared to some I may have had it rough - compared to others I had it easy. I was unable (even now) to cry for myself yet I could cry for Genie and Michael.

I witnessed much racism whilst in various forms of social care - particularly towards mixed race (Afro/Anglo) children. Not only from both black and white children but also from white carers. I spent much time with the mixed race kids hence saw this first-hand. Often in the 1960s and early 70s white single mothers had their 'half-caste bastards' removed from the safety of their care and placed in horrific situations. Many were farmed out for adoption: however not all - not the 'naughty ones'.

Genie, Michael, my sister and I resided in foster care - I picture in East

OUTSIDE THE LINES

Ham. Genie and Michael were both mixed raced - slightly older than me and attended secondary school. At night the man of the house would take either one of them into the room at the end of the hall.

The first time Michael was taken he was compliant. Once in the room I heard him cry - scream - shout - beg - choke - gag - throw up and keep on screaming. The next time he resisted being taken, so he was dragged. After two/three weeks he no longer resisted - he did what he was told - all that was heard was whimpering. The man did not make a sound. Michael stopped speaking, ate little and lost much weight. No one said a word about it.

Although we never spoke of it, one at a time we were all taken into the room for a 'talking to' by the man.

I was told - "Never talk about what you have seen to anyone - do you understand?" I said nothing - saying nothing was the wrong answer. He took off his belt, doubled it over and belted me around the face. "Do you understand?" I understood.

I had not realised that Genie was also regularly being taken into 'the room'. She made no sound and there was no resistance. I found out one night when I got up to go to the toilet; I could hear him whispering to her - "Your brown skin is beautiful - so smooth - open your legs wider: I said wider!"

I ran back into my bedroom and cried. Later I heard the water running in the bathroom - Genie was scrubbing herself…

Uncle Leslie

1969 - Although the intention was never to return, we had returned from Australia (you need to read the first book). When we left my parents had given away or sold all of our household belongings. Much was given to my mum's sister Myra and her husband Leslie. They lived in Harlow and on occasions when we visited them, on the car journey, my dad would sing the song 'Little Boxes' - insinuating that all the houses in the new development looked like small boxes. It was a giant depressing modern housing estate. Leslie was a foreman at Plessey (a British-based international electronics, defence and telecommunications company) - Myra I have no idea about. Neither seemed too smart.

Upon our return from Australia Myra and Leslie did not offer to return any of the household goods which they were given.

To me Leslie kind of looked a bit like a 1950s Teddy boy. Loose-fitting jacket - black suede chukka boots - wide trousers with turn-ups - greased back hair and a bit slow on the uptake. He liked to take electrical goods apart and then would struggle to put them back together. If he ever came around to visit my dad would say - "Quick, hide your toys just in case Leslie tries to fix them."

He loved to fiddle with new gadgets, particularly cameras; he considered himself an expert. My dad could not stand him and referred to Myra and Lesley as 'the enemy'.

My mum/dad/sister and I were all staying at my mum's house in Redbridge (to be honest I had little understanding of the ins and outs of our housing situation).

Leslie was in my dad's face regarding nothing in particular. My dad was his usual reserved self - Leslie was extremely agitated and animated. My dad knew

OUTSIDE THE LINES

1953 - Myra & Leslie

it was not going to end well. He decided to put my sister and me in the back of the car and leave. Leslie tried to obstruct him; my dad simply walked around him and got into the car.

He started the engine and then wound down the window. "I see that you're still wearing my tie!" He then wound the window back up and proceeded to back out of the driveway laughing to himself.

Leslie was banging hard on the window. "Get out of the fucking car. I'm gonna smash your face in."

My dad drove off still laughing.

Later I asked. "Why did you let him get away with that?"
"Where would the fun be in getting out and knocking his block off - there is no long-term satisfaction in that"

This is where my bad-minded humour came from…

'Ball Of Confusion'
1970 (10 years old) - my sister purchased Motown Chartbusters Vol.5: Ball Of Confusion was on the LP. I listened to it intently over and over waiting for certain parts - listened intently and analysed. I had no idea why - I didn't even understand what the lyrics referred to - but I knew it was special. Fifty years later my own music is still influenced by the production of Norman Whitfield and the Temptations are still my favourite band…

Summer School
1970 - We were moving permanently from Whitechapel to Redbridge. My mum had been living there since our return from Australia. The final move actually took eighteen months - going back and forth from the flat in Whitechapel to the three-bedroom house in Redbridge.

I never questioned it but I suppose that my parents were not together at the

OUTSIDE THE LINES

time. My sister and I had already spent some time in Redbridge and attended Redbridge Junior School directly opposite our house. I quite liked it - to me it was like living out in the country - there were open fields and a river.

The official narrative was that the move was to keep me out of and away from trouble. I was not buying that - I was trouble. My mum rejoiced in the fact that we were moving to a predominantly Jewish area (the East End by this time was very mixed) - she wanted her kids to experience her Jewish culture.

My dad on the other hand was nonchalant; he took people at face value liking few and trusting none.

This story is not PC, yet of its time and I was 10 years old.

To acclimatise us to our new situation my sister and I were sent away for six weeks to a Jewish summer school in Folkestone - to get a feel for 'the culture'. My mother rejoiced and my dad was glad to have us out of the way.

Nice Jewish kids - naughty East End skinhead - a recipe for disaster. It turned out that the Jewish kids dressed the same as me - the skinhead culture seemed present beyond the East End. They were as naughty and as rough/tough as me - some even more so.

My friend David came along but he went home after a week because he was homesick, which kind of left me very much on my own. I befriended a few older girls which resulted in me showing off; jumping from a twenty foot high sea wall onto the stony beach and cutting my hands on the sharp pebbles - running into the sea with my Levi's on and them shrinking on me as I lay in the sun - throwing up at Dreamland Fairground in Margate after riding 'The New Tom Jones' - a ride that went 70mph forward stopped and then 70mph backwards - I had three goes.

In the evenings the teenagers usually played reggae and Motown records and danced. I liked to slow dance with and kiss the older girls to the French song 'Je T'Aime' - many had older boyfriends; this did not bode so well with them. There was this one kid Simon, he must have been 13 years old, who regularly threw me to the floor, straddled my chest and continuously punched me in the chin. After a while the blows to my chin would cause a sharp pain in my ears and I would blackout: he seemed to know what he was doing. Whilst one of these incidents was occurring his girlfriend (Susan Cohen from Elephant & Castle) came up behind him and whacked him across the head with a rounders bat. We both then went out onto the playing fields. She pushed me back onto a shallow hill and laid on top of me and we started kissing: she also rubbed and pushed her hips into mine - I had no idea what that bit was all about.

Francine Barden was a nice Jewish girl a few years older than me and a hardened skinhead. She insisted on becoming my girlfriend. Now, she knew how to get into serious trouble and was eventually sent home. In the meantime we had great laughs together. She too took me to the playing fields and pushed me back onto the shallow hill, lay on top of me kissing my lips and rubbed and pushed her hips into mine. I had to ask - and was told - "Oh!" I relaxed and began to enjoy it. After summer school we kept in contact, she lived in Southgate - where the fuck was Southgate? Due to the distance between our homes we would meet at Battersea Fun Fair. That is all I can remember - except for my mum once meeting her. "She's old enough to be your aunty" - which became a family joke.

There was this French dude Yves - 12 years old and a bully who really fancied himself as a hard nut (wearing red flares). He would often fuck about and embarrass me in front of girls knowing that I could do nothing about it. Spat at

OUTSIDE THE LINES

me - tripped me up - slapped me around the face - snapped my braces against my back - pulled my trousers down: every boy's nightmare.

One day I walked into the billiards room and accidentally 'disturbed' Yves' game of snooker. He picked up the cue, held it like a spear and propelled it towards my head narrowly missing my eye and penetrating the skin above my left eyebrow. I have not thought about this since the occurrence - I just checked and can feel the indentation and have a very faint scar.

"You French Jewish cunt" (sorry I was 10 years old). I picked up the cue, gripped with both hands in the middle and rammed it into his stomach, kicked him in the bollocks and then smashed the cue right across the centre of his head. He fell - I continuously stamped on his head - ribs - arms - legs.

"I am from the East End!"
"I am from the East End!"
"I am from the East End!"
"I am from the East End!"
"I am from the East End!"
"I am from the East End!"

I went to bed with blood trickling down my face - the wound turned out to be superficial. Yves on the other hand was taken by ambulance to the hospital.

The next day I was sent home, not for the violence, but for calling him a 'French Jewish cunt'. It was actually for the best as I intended repeating my actions each and every time I saw the 'French Jewish cunt' - with his fucking poofy red Lionel Blairs…

Redbridge

The 1970s - I enjoyed my time living in Redbridge and embraced the surrounding areas - Wanstead - Gants Hill - Ilford - Barkingside.

I was a Whitechapelite - rough and boisterous - the instigator of much trouble and fighting. I was a bit of a loner and often lonely. I had few friends and trusted no one. I was often wrongly accused, victimised and picked on - a crap I did not give.

The long 1970s summers were lovely and maybe the time of my happiest memories. I loved the long walk to Valentines Park Lido (possibly the coldest swimming pool in the world). I would stroll along with my swimming trunks under my Levi 501s (while most still wore Lionels) - Italian loafers (sans socks) and my Lacoste polo shirt tucked into the waistband of my jeans - I never actually put it on because it interfered with my tanning. I needed no towel as I rarely swam - if I did dip myself in the pool I would merely dry off in the sun.

It was about this time that I got to grips with reading - I guess I was 15/16. I used to carry my book to the pool and bask in the sun while reading. Due to dyslexia as I get older my reading skills are diminishing. On a positive note - since mastering the computer I am able to express my true thoughts through writing: previously I preferred silence regarding my views upon the world.

I loved to read biographies and factual books - my favourites being:
The Autobiography of Malcolm X
Seize The Time
Bury My Heart At Wounded Knee
Hell's Angel
I Know Why The Caged Bird Sings
I could go on - there are many more yet these were the first.

OUTSIDE THE LINES

I had to catch up on the cult Richard Allen fictional books of my youth:
Skinhead
Suedehead
Boot Boys
Etcetera

Plus a bit of culture:
Watership Down
Animal Farm
1984

I also discovered Harold Robbins - whom I now realise is my main influence as a writer: the way he visually put me in the moment:
Never Love A Stranger
A Stone For Danny Fisher
79 Park Avenue
Circa 1978 I stayed in St. Tropez aboard Harold Robbin's yacht - in hindsight I may have been a bit naïve.

I digress - back to Redbridge and surrounding areas.

Tiffany's (Ilford Palais) with its plastic palm trees, awful cover band (The Nocturnes) and the ultraviolet lights. I was 11 when I first went on a Saturday afternoon for under 13s. Reggae - Motown - girls - slick clothing: I was in my element.

1974 - Tuesday nights at Tiffany's - soul and funk. Banjo controlled the door thus I was guaranteed to get in - even wearing sandals (sans socks). The music was exhilarating. I would watch the dancers twisting their bodies - dipping - swaying all night long. Similar to what I now see on vintage Soul

1970

Train footage: Afros - flares - big collars - platform shoes. I comprehended movement - I could participate and fit in - I was noticed. I became friends with the best dancers - the very best being Sammy Greason. This gave me access to girls - I only liked the ones who danced well and now I could dance with them. Strangely it was only ever black girls that gave me any attention. I was too shy to speak first, hence had to wait until they engaged me on the dance floor.

1976 - Tiffany's Sunday nights - soul and funk and that awful band The Nocturnes. It was on one of these Sunday nights that the embarrassing 'who are you the fucking Levi Kid' incident occurred (story told in previous book).

Then there was the legendry Lacy Lady in Seven Kings that launched so many new styles and that many claim to have attended - a tiny club - too small to accommodate so many claimants.

OUTSIDE THE LINES

1977 - My Membership Card

Room at The Top Club
HIGH ROAD ILFORD ESSEX
01-478-5588

1977 - Tuesday nights - The Room At The Top - Ilford High Road above the Harrison and Gibson furniture store. Infamous for its mixture of gangsters and dancers: dancing the night away to the latest disco music. Situated on the tenth floor - access by lift - that was if one could get past the aggressive racist detritus on the door. Alternatively we would bunk in via the fire escape: an epic upward journey. Upon occasion I have also had to escape to the street down that long never-ending winding stairway.

The Ilford High Road shops - a veritable feast of department stores, chain stores and swanky fashion boutiques. In the early 70s there was Byrite (very rated in the early days) and the more upmarket Granditers. Both stores a must for any self-respecting skinhead or suedehead in the need of a tonic suit - a pair of Levi Sta Press - Brutus or Ben Sherman shirt. Granditers also sold shoes: Loafers - Nobles - Royals - Brogues.

The High Road also boasted a Selfridges and on Station Road the famous Bodgers department store (which I believe has just recently closed) with its shiny slot machine Indian Motorcycle ride in the huge toy department. Every boy had to have a go - although it did not do much besides rock back and forth

Fullwell Cross Library

with lights flashing and making slight motorbike noises.

My favourite was the Bronx Shop - way down the high street, past the town hall, past Tiffany's and further on past the ABC cinema. It was an emporium of Italian style - fine gauge fully fashioned knitwear - bench-made shoes - 32" wide Oxford Bags - spearpoint collared gabardine shirts. I managed to secure a Saturday job circa 1975 - but was sacked for spending all day trying on the clothes.

Barkingside: with its modern library, swimming pool (at the time both state of the art) and Rossi's ice cream parlour. I spent many evenings sitting alone in the library looking at books, particularly The Cat In The Hat and Little Black Sambo - both had highly colourful imagery: I was unable to read them.

OUTSIDE THE LINES

Fullwell Cross Swimming Baths

Regarding Helen Bannerman's Little Black Sambo - although unquestioned and deemed acceptable in its day - totally racist in name - yet only now unacceptable. However, in its defence, the boy depicted in the book is historically documented as the first black literary hero: thoughtful and extremely intelligent - a winner. He outwitted the tigers (turning them into butter) and always carried an umbrella to protect him from both the sun and rain. The name of the book is greatly unfortunate, yet the sentiment most positive - at least that is how I viewed it as a 6-year-old child.

Many an evening also spent alone in the Fullwell Cross swimming pool - although I could not actually swim - then after onto Rossi's ice cream parlour for a 99 (ice cream in a cone with a flake stuck in it).

Yes - Redbridge and surrounding areas have warm memories for me…

The Education System
When I was young life and the class divide was simple:
Private school: upper class
Grammar school: middle class
Secondary modern school: lower class ('no hoper').

Then the government created the Comprehensive School system and no one knew where he or she stood, nor whom he or she could trust: it was a social bear pit.

Now we have 'Academies' which have little to do with education - a system of control and ticking boxes - if you do not fit in you are out...

My Experience
For one to discuss the complex historic cycles of English racism one must have a comprehensive understanding. This comes from experience. It can be felt and smelt - xenophobia oozes from suburban perspective.

The late 60s early 70s skinhead culture was a combination of Jamaican style and music - homogenised with a British working-class attitude - unique to the quagmire of Britain's inner cities.

Where I came from - the East End of London - the majority of the kids that I knew were skinheads - black/white/Asian. It was a style - a fashion statement. We had no political views nor prejudices - we were kids: we were not our parents.

It was the skinhead movement that first brought urban black and white kids together in the playground: a sacred new and exciting bond emerged.

OUTSIDE THE LINES

Saying all that - I clearly remember East End skinheads in the (pre ICF - Inter City Firm: Google it) Southbank throwing bananas at West Ham's Clyde Best and making monkey chants at him.

Skinheads were from a cross-section of society hence of course there were many racist skinheads ready to spread hate and hostility towards minorities.

'Little Britain' was/is and always will be a cesspit of racist xenophobia - unlike the free and easy melting pot experienced by 1960/70s inner-city kids. Many of the suburban skinheads were no more than racist thugs.

Capitalism thrives on pitting the lower classes against each other. For its continued survival capitalism needs the working class demonisation of minorities…

Crime And Capitalism
Crime is demographic: not colour - race - religion specific. In Southall the crime is predominantly Asian - Surbiton white - Hackney black etc ~ etc. This also applies to knife crime - however, knife crime predominately affects those forced to the bottom of the social dung-heap and capitalism thrives upon the existence of the 'social dung-heap'…

Sexual Education
1972 - My mother was again in hospital - or as often described the 'Nut-House'. I was placed within foster care in Ilford. A large cold house with many simple bare rooms: bed - table - cupboard - drawers - wooden floor. Five kids resided there; all with our own room. Brenda, the lady of the house, was a harsh loveless woman who always wore her black hair in a tight bun.

Memoirs Of A Naughty Boy #2

This was where I first met Marcie - we later spent time in Doctor Barnardo's together. Slim - attractive - dark skinned - deep wild brown eyes: her hair - always badly braided or inadequately combed. Two years older than me, yet we gelled. We laughed - played - danced - eventually had sex together.

Marcie and I shared many of our early life experiences - people thought that she led me astray but I was already astray.

It was a hot summer - Marcie was in her bedroom (our bedrooms were the coolest places in the house) - outside the temperature was soaring in the high 80s. I went upstairs to sit alone in my own room. I heard noises coming from Marcie's quarters: low moans. Without knocking I walked in. She was laying on her back - on her bed - skirt up - legs open - knees bent - hand moving in her knickers. I did not understand, I just stood and watched.

Marcie did not interrupt what she was doing - she stared into my eyes. Suddenly she stopped - stood up and removed her knickers - then sat on the edge of the bed: skirt still up - smooth long brown legs again open. I had never seen her like this - I had never seen anyone like this.

"Do you like it?" I did not know, thus was silent - I may have nodded. She looked into my eyes and touched herself there. "Touch it." I touched it. It was damp and warm: unfamiliarly musky. She pushed two of my fingers inside her and manoeuvred my hand back and forth: I remained silent yet compliant.

"Use your tongue - lick me."
I pulled back.
"Please do it - I want to know how it feels."

I knelt between her legs and licked - it was bitter and very wet - she rubbed

OUTSIDE THE LINES

herself with her fingers.
"Faster!"

She thrust forward with her hips - gripping my head with both hands. My lips were hurting from the hardness of her pubic bone. She pushed and ground. Harder - faster - wetter: the taste more bitter. She shuddered, sighed then stopped. I felt a strange new sensation in my pants - then dampness.

We did not speak - in fact we did not speak of it until a year later in Barnardos. We repeated this act most days - often more than once. I do not know if it damaged me or opened me - however, I became very popular with Marcie's friends. Unfortunately 12 weeks after finding solace my father collected me - my mother was once again 'stable' - although after shock treatment she had no idea who I was…

Marcie
Between my first sexual encounter with Marcia May in 1972 and until she was raped and subsequently killed herself in 1975 we had the most amazing times together. (Rape story depicted in previous book).

Circa 1974 - I had been living back with my parents in Redbridge for three years but I still regularly visited and hung out with Marcie - either at Barnardo's or we would meet up to go on an adventure: I was hooked on Marcie. These adventures, whether sexual, dangerous or just plain fun, may seem dark to many - to us it was what we did and usually enjoyed every minute of it with much laughter. Upon reflection it was after Marcie died that I stopped smiling and laughing. I definitely spoke much less - there seemed to be very few people that fathomed me.

Living Quarters Doctor Barnardos (Now A Plush Housing Estate)

We got up to things that some would never understand. We were damaged children - we thrived upon our damage and exploited our own vulnerability before anyone else could.

We usually headed uptown. My favourite adventures were around Earls Court or South Kensington. This area seemed to have a mystical Dickensian regal air about it - a warm sensation of grandeur and riches. An area that was always easy to steal from or pull off some dastardly scam. We were very naughty - in fact we were horrible kids. People would treat us to a meal or a drink and all we wanted to do was rip them off.

OUTSIDE THE LINES

1974

I loved going into Biba on Kensington High Street. A truly 1920s spiritual experience - like being transported back in time. Everything about it was weird - the building (Derry & Toms - later Barkers) with its Deco masonry and high ceilings - the decor - the people - the clothes (often just piled up on the floor): a fairy-tale land.

It was the trips to Soho that were dubious: Marcie had studied the sex trade and the easy money to be made by just allowing a man to have his way with her. Of course I went along with it. We would have money - no thoughts beyond that.

Marcie was not just looking for a few bob, she had really studied this subject matter and hanging around Soho gave her the info needed to tap into the real money. She made connections - a pretty young black girl had value to older white men - the taboo.

We found out that there were Gentlemen's clubs in the Strand and St. James where wealthy businessmen and MPs spent their leisure time (we had no idea what an MP was). Whilst staying in town the gentlemen had their own quarters.

I was not 100% comfortable with this - out of my depth. "What difference to you? You ain't gotta do nuthink!" True enough - I did not have to do 'nuthink'!

Sometimes I would wait for hours in the street for her to return with £££. We would have a slap up meal, go to late night pictures and then get a taxi home. Good times.

Within a period of two months she got more acquainted with the gentlemen - they treated us well. Often men would look at me and whisper to her, her reply was always "No!" I had no idea at the time what they were referring to. She was looking out for me, yet had little regard for herself. Marcie was older and smarter than me.

As it all became more familiar we became confident and felt quite safe. Marcie always insisted I go with her - like a puppy I tagged along. By this time I no longer had to wait in the cold for her return; I was welcome in the gentlemen's quarters where I would sit very bored and wait. I often heard what was going on in the bedroom - most of it was quite strange to me. We no longer had any other adventures - it was now all about selling Marcie's body. 'A means to an end' - neither of us knew what that meant but she kept saying it.

OUTSIDE THE LINES

Brooks' Club - St James's Street

One night it was very different. Marcie was introduced to some right poncey scumbag - a definite wrongun: then again they were all wronguns. We were invited to his rooms. Marcie received her fee which she handed to me. The man asked if I would like to watch - she said "NO!"

This all felt wrong - I was confused - I wanted her to leave with me but I had to sit and wait. Anxiety knotting my stomach - breath short - heart palpitations: an adrenaline overload.

"No jonny no entry - you know that."
I could hear him insisting - demanding. I could hear her agitation.
"No fucking way - are you fucking mad!"

I was crapping myself.
Her voice became muffled. "B ~ B ~ B - help!"

Fuck it - I pushed open the door and cautiously stepped in. I almost laughed with relief when I saw his skinny pale legs and small willy. He was trying to shove it up her bum - the condom was clearly too big. I startled him, his willy got even smaller and Marcie punched him in the balls. Of course before leaving she took his wallet.

We left laughing - more of a nervous laugh than one of fun - relieved and wanting to go home. In the cab I literally begged her not to do this anymore - she agreed: she was already over it…

NF
Circa 1973 - I guess we were now on the suedehead side of being skinheads - longer hair - smarter shoes - neat Tonic suits - penny collared Brutus shirts - Fair Isle jumpers.

There were about eleven of us. At 13 I was the youngest - the eldest being 17. My cousin Albert - our leader - had just turned 15. We were a typical East End gang (group of boisterous friends) - black - white - Asian - Jewish - Muslim. We did not feel the differences - nor care. More importantly we were neighbours, we naturally played together as we grew up conjointly on the streets of East London.

I know it was spring because I was wearing a white Fred Perry tennis shirt with navy and red striped tipped collar. It was market day and we were hanging on the corner of Bethnal Green Road and Brick Lane - where we met every Sunday morning: bored and looking for mischief.

OUTSIDE THE LINES

Brick Lane was not the trendy quaint little vintage art and crafts market that we know today - with fancy restaurants and expensive chocolate: it was a busy hustling bustling market place. Vendors - pickpockets - antiquities - conmen (Find The Lady) - fruit and veg - bric-a-brac - exotic animals on Club Row. Spreading all the way to The Waste (Whitechapel Road) - Petticoat Lane - Columbia Row: five thriving East End markets in the 1960s 70s and 80s.

For the last three/four weeks the National Front had not been out selling the 'National Front News'. In my dad's words a 'racist rag' - of course I had no idea what that meant nor actually what the NF were all about. All I knew was that locally no one liked them. The NF members I saw were hardened skinheads - not the well dressed ones - but the ones we referred to as 'boot boys': the football hooligans - all boots and braces.

This particular Sunday the NF was there in force - at least twenty of them. Big dirty blokes with long sideboards and unpolished boots. We were all up bright and early waiting to see what amusement Albert was going to come up with.

"Come on B."
Up I jumped from sitting on the floor outside the shop that sold fishing tackle, airguns and catapults (123 Bethnal Green Road).
"Yous lot stay here - just me and B - none of you spades nor pakis - you'll give the game away."
He laughed - typical East End irony.
"What we gonna do?"
"Dunno yet."
We strolled over the road and through the casually standing NF - right up to the kid selling the 'National Front News'.
"Givus a paper mate."
"One bob."

Memoirs Of A Naughty Boy #2

123 Bethnal Green Road

"There ya go." Handing him 5p.

Albert threw the paper on the floor and offers the kid another shilling for another newspaper. Uhh Oh. Albert was pretty tasty - but I, although fearless, was not - well at least compared to the hard nuts we hung around with and clearly no match for these gorillas.

Until my son was born I had no real comprehension of fear.

OUTSIDE THE LINES

"Are you 'avin' a fuckin' laugh mate?"
"Yeah - but what the fuck are gonna do about it - cunt!"

Now I was not so fearless - indeed cacking myself. The group of gorillas were gathering around us - nonetheless our own little firm was gathering around them and shouting abuse. The fracas incited a few stallholders to run over - the next thing I knew all hell broke loose. No longer a few kids taunting the NF but hardcore East End NF hating market traders getting their hands dirty.

As I literally crawled out of the affray, unscathed, I saw Albert's dad - my uncle Frank - steaming in (that was where Albert got his craziness from) - Frank was a fucking psychopath. Much blood was spilt - funnily enough much of it was Albert's - who got the crap beaten out of him before the stallholders came to his rescue. Personally I was only interested in self-preservation and just wanted to get out of there. Albert was happy to stay and fight - no matter what the odds nor the outcome.

When my dad found out he gave me a long and logical lecture regarding possible alternative outcomes of the situation - although we both knew he would have loved to of been there.

I hardly saw Albert after that - he had a fascination with guns. In his late teens - apparently by accident - he blew his own head off with a sawn-off shotgun. Not much was ever said to me about it - (this answers the frequently asked question - 'what happened to Albert' - following on from a story in my previous book)...

Paul 'Trouble' Anderson

As we get older we lose more and more friends - the secret is not to lose oneself.

Our paths first crossed in 1973 - for a very short period I was placed in a children's home in Hackney. My mum was sick and my dad elsewhere - same story different home.

My prized possession was my Phillips cassette player - the one with the huge piano key controls - one of the only things that my dad ever bought for me. I recorded all of my Reggae, Motown and James Brown records onto cassettes - the records were safe in my parents' house: easily 'misplaced' in some of the institutions that I was shipped out to.

I often sat on the front step of the building listening to my music: a black kid around my age would sometimes come and sit next to me and also listen. His name was Paul - we were not friends and rarely exchanged words. "What's this one?" I would reply with the name of the song and the artist. Paul had a good energy.

I next saw Paul in 1974 at the Tottenham Royal. I could not get in through the front door because I was wearing sandals (sans socks) - this happened to me quite a lot - so I bunked in through the back door.

The size of the Tottenham Royal was overwhelming - it was built as a tram shed at the turn of the 20th Century - a huge space. The building was packed with hot sweaty dancers; moving and swaying to 'Express' by B.T. Express - I had never seen so many black kids in one place.

I tried to find my friends but found myself watching two boys competing on the dance floor - not my style of dance - it was rigid and controlled, yet very

OUTSIDE THE LINES

skilled: quite mesmerising. Recognising Paul as one of the dancers I pushed my way to the front hoping to catch his eye. When he saw me he stopped dancing, came straight over and grabbed my arm, pulling me to a quieter place by the wall. We did not say much - Paul was very warm towards me and gave me a hug - I was a bit out of my comfort zone but appreciated the camaraderie.

I bumped into him every so often in various clubs - not many words uttered - yet a bond was forming. We spoke more in depth at the 100 Club circa 1976 - we spoke more at Crackers later that year. By this time I hardly went to Crackers: Mark Roman had left to play at Jaws (formally The Lively Lady) in Leytonstone and I followed. The new DJ at Crackers was George Power - although he played the latest disco music I preferred Mark Roman's style of DJ'ing: much funkier - more diverse.

Paul was now George Power's 'Boxboy'; he also did the warm-up session. By this time I had put two and two together - I realised that Paul was 'Paul Anderson' - whose name was often whispered in clubs in regard to his dancing - he had made quite a name for himself.

This is how our friendship intermittently continued - the odd word here and there in loud - hot - sweaty - dark clubs.

1984 - I was DJ'ing at Black Market (The Wag) - I put on a long record and rushed to the toilet. As I went in there was this dude coming out that I recognised - being a bit spaced out from LSD I was unsure of myself. He had short locks which were unfamiliar to me - however, I knew that I knew him. "Paul?"
He looked at me strange.
"Yeah?"
We hugged and then I had to rush off to quickly pee and then get back to the

Memoirs Of A Naughty Boy #2

2014 - PTA @ Sharpeye - Agar Grove - Collecting Hat

OUTSIDE THE LINES

2015 -
PTA @ Sharpeye
- Agar Grove

decks before the record ended.

1985 - Paul was playing to a tiny audience in the foyer of the Scala cinema (Kings X). I listened to what he was dropping - a similar take on 70s funk to what Lascelle and I were playing. I went to speak to him; he gave me a warm smile and hug. He was not doing too well and had a few personal issues that he needed to deal with to get back on his feet. I gave him my number and asked him to call me. A few days later he called - I asked him if he wanted to play with Lascelle and me at The Cat In The Hat. He was happy to. I decided not to play for a few weeks and let Paul and Lascelle get on with it - I was content just to dance. What Paul did that was unique was to mix and scratch funk records together: not an easy task.

*2014 - PTA -
Bussey Building*

A month later Lascelle went back to the Wag to play at Black Market - so I started playing again. Paul would always turn up late - plonk a slab of hash on the corner of each deck - one for me one for him - and proceeded to roll spliffs all night long. I was often so stoned that I could only select the records I wanted to play and get Paul to play them for me: in his own inimitable style.

After The Cat In The Hat closed I stopped DJ'ing to concentrate on Diana Brown And The Brothers - Paul went on to become London's Premiere House DJ.

After that I only really hooked up with him at the Soul II Soul parties - Sundays in the Africa Centre: when that closed I hardly saw him at all.

OUTSIDE THE LINES

Flyer Designed By Marco Cairns (Duffer)

Many years later he became ill and contacted me to play (in his stead) at his Wednesday night funk club in Camden - 'Back To My Roots' - I did so without hesitation. He had to have a major operation to combat cancer - the recovery process was long and painful - yet for a while combat it he did.

We were now speaking on the phone regularly, often about the music that Paul was producing or wanted to produce and the book he badly needed to write. Alas, although I offered many times to help him write it, the book did not get written.

He worked hard but his health was waning - he often spoke of tiredness and pain but could not stop working - living his life was what kept him going.

We spoke every three/four weeks - I felt guilty about this because he would always call me - I avoided calling him because I knew his calls could take up to two hours or more in length. Paul could really talk - talking about whatever came into his head - this I now regret…

The Funeral.
December 2018 - Personally I struggled to see it as a celebration - although I do realise for many celebration was a comfort.

I am not man who is familiar with church hence sat at the back on my own - quite lost. Thankfully Jazzie B picked up on my discomfort. "B - come sit with me and Efua (his wife)." He led me to the front pews and indicated to sit next to Norman Jay - Norman and I have not seen eye to eye for a long while. We instinctively shook hands. Jazzie exclaimed - "It's time to be strong together."

I felt a strange solace in sitting next to Norman, feeling his loss was equal to mine. When directed to hold one's neighbour's hand, we indeed firmly gripped hands - letting the tears freely flow…

OUTSIDE THE LINES

December 2018 - PTA's Funeral - With Norman Jay

What Is Life Without Death Or Death Without Re-Birth…?
As one life ends another begins
The essence of life passed on
Breathing life into the newborn
The cycle continues to recycle for an eternity
Life moves on
Forever changing
Until in turn it is our time to pass
A new life will commence…
(Barrie Sharpe December 2018)

Memoirs Of A Naughty Boy #2

The Funfair

1973 - Like most kids I had a fascination with the fairground. The danger - the smell - the reggae music - the candyfloss - the hot dogs - the mixture of people and cultures - the Waltzer - the bumper cars. The cool teenagers that rode the back of the dodgems impressed me - I too wished to become a roustabout at the funfair and ride the dodgems.

It was Easter Bank Holiday and the fair had again returned to Wanstead Flats. My best friend Eugene Kuti and I secured ourselves jobs to ride the cars and collect the fare money.

Wanstead Flats was (probably still is) common land where people had historical rights to collect wood, cut turf for fuel and allow their livestock to graze (dating back to the Magna Carta).

We wore our made to measure thirty two inch wide Oxford Bags, South Sea Bubble V-neck jumpers - topped off with our ten hole cherry red steel toed Doctor Martens boots.

The upside was that we would look cool, be able to chat up the girls and steal as much money as our deep pockets could hold. The downside was the fine dust created by the electric conductor at the top of the car's back-pole, connecting to the metal mesh grid that covered the roof of the arena - (this is also the reason for the smell of the dodgems) - our filthy skin dried - lips cracked - our hair caked in dust - our clothes stunk.

There were plastic lensed lights protruding at the back of the cars - when being flash, riding on the thick rubber bumper, every time the cars crashed into one another my shins were smashed against the lights. After a while each bump became agony and my shins swelled up like bruised sausages. I was also run over many times as I jumped from car to car to collect the 10p fares.

Although I ended the weekend with plenty of stolen ten pence pieces my shins were damaged beyond recognition. Still today if I knock them even slightly they sting like hell.

It has recently brought my attention that my left shin has possibly had nine minor fractures and my right thirteen - some may have been fractures upon fractures…

Lucky
1974 - Lenny Aylen (a key player in the Wanstead firm) - "You don't know how lucky you are Barnet." All the geezers at that time would call me Barnet (Barnet fair/hair) because I had my hair in the latest short style, whereas they all still wore their hair long.

"About six months ago me, ---, --- and --- (three names that now conveniently escape me) saw you walking down Leytonstone High Road late one night on your own - we were gonna shiv you up. You're fucking lucky son, we decided you weren't worth it."
"Why?"
"You had a ruck with my little brother and needed a slap."

His 'little' brother Gary - 2 years older, much bigger and had actually beat the crap out of me. The thing is I knew he was serious - these four gentlemen were movers and shakers in the original ICF.

Earlier that year I was hanging outside the Plough and Harrow on Leytonstone High Road - a notoriously violent pub which just happened to have a great DJ - with Andy Pendry and Mark Ilsly ('Ils'). My school friend Gary Aylen tore out of the pub and grabbed Ils around the throat. Somehow Ils got away and a chase ensued - I do not know why I got involved but I did - I chased after the pair trying to stop Gary from catching Ils - Gary's anger turned on me. Fortunately a girl named (I think) Gill stepped in.

Gill was tall - skinny - short blond hair - not too pretty: I did not particularly like conventionally pretty girls. She was as hard as nails with a few older brothers that had a reputation on the street - no one messed with her. She was always around, I now realise that she fancied me, at the time I was naïve. She called me Muhammad (Ali) - as every time she saw me I was in a fight of some sort.

Back to the pub: Gary was fuming - his temper now directed at me. Apparently Ils had been hovering around Gary's ex-girlfriend - Sally Swainson. Sally was in the year above me at school - I used to hang around with her and her friends at lunchtimes.

"You need to keep your fucking nose out of my business."
"I ain't scared of you - I shouldn't have to be - I am much younger." I cockily replied.
Bunny Jackson piped up. "Kick 'is fuckin' head in." For some reason he hated me.

Bang ~ bang ~ bang - I tried to fight back but it was fruitless - Tony Capon (one of the Wanstead firm) eventually stepped in and stopped the fight. Gill was there giving Gary, who was still fuming, plenty of verbal.

"You younger lot ain't got no fuckin' respect - we look out for you!" Winkle (Gary's close mate) exclaimed.

"You are fucking lucky son, we decided you weren't worth it" - said Lenny…

OUTSIDE THE LINES

The Big Fight On Wanstead Flats
Autumn 1974 - me and a couple of friends had gone to Aldersbrook Hall Youth Club in Manor Park. We may have seemed a bit flash in our made to measure Oxford bags and expensive Toppers crepe wedge shoes. We were off our manor and knew very few of the kids attending - a bit out of our comfort zone.

My friends Gary Davis and Sammy Imber were off doing their own thing whilst I was dancing in the little disco area. As always I brought a few of my own 7" reggae records along. The DJ put on 'One Step Beyond' by Prince Buster and I got into a shuffling competition with two black kids with huge Afros: one I now know to have been Dennis Elcock (RIP). We danced close trying to trip each other up - hankies out - tricks performed - I made my point. We laughed and shook hands and I was off to talk to a girl - that was a mistake. She was the girlfriend of one of the local hard kids (I did not know his name) and he was not having it. He barged into me and a minor scuffle ensued. Outside quite a few local boys surrounded my friends and me. With the odds not in our favour we talked our way out of being taken onto Wanstead Flats and having the crap beaten out of us. Besides we were wearing our best clothes and I was holding my records.

The next week I returned with a tasty little crew - though as soon as we got off the bus we realised that we were outnumbered and not so tasty. We ran across the road to get on the 101 bus, that was just pulling up, back to Wanstead. Even the hardest amongst us were pushing to get onto the bus whilst we were pelted with mud and stones.

Arriving in Wanstead I went into The George pub hoping to gather recruits from the heavyweight Wanstead firm. I saw Paul Wheatley (Winkle) and Gary Aylen. Whilst telling them of our plight Gary's older brother Lenny came over and listened - "Next week we will go and do 'em" - not because he particularly liked me but was always up for a physical altercation.

The next Wednesday I turned up at The George with a small crew. In the pub an army of at least thirty had gathered, these were not kids, well not to me - they were mostly in their late teens.

The plan was that my friends and I get the bus to Wanstead Flats and they all follow in cars - we were to be the bait.

Twelve of us jumped off the bus and crossed the road to where our foes were gathered - knowing that we were heavily outnumbered yet confident of the outcome. We were surrounded in a circle - somehow my friends had integrated into the crowd and I was left in the middle to face this huge kid - as wide as he was tall - with a mass of red hair. It was already past the point of no return and our backup was nowhere to be seen. This was it - him and me - he was going to kill me. As he approached I launching myself off the ground spanking him in the face with all I had - which was not enough. I continued to punch - achieving very little.

Out of the ether came Dave Kuti - flying through the air like a flash of lightning. Dave was quite distinctive: the only mixed race guy in the firm and he always wore a Queens Park Rangers football Jersey: the same worn by his musical hero Alex Harvey of 'The Sensational Alex Harvey Band'. Dave was holding a tennis racket which he wrapped around my attacker's head. Mayhem occured as the entire Wanstead firm got into action. It was like a movie; fists - feet - dust flying: leaving many motionless on the ground. We were completely triumphant - however, this was not the end.

Over the next week rumours of an even bigger firm were now involved - 'the

OUTSIDE THE LINES

Wanstead firm and Barrie Sharpe were all dead'. I was absolutely shitting myself as I had now been named. Every time I left the house I thought that they were waiting for me - if a car slowed down my heart skipped a beat - of course they had no idea where I even lived.

The following Wednesday, back in The George as arranged, we were going back to 'finish it'. But this time there was only six of the Wanstead firm in the pub - all still game for a ruck: though me - not so much. We all jumped into the back of a Ford Escort van and off we went to Wanstead Flats - to 'finish it'.

We parked on the far side of the vast grassy fields. In the distance I could see them: lots and lots of them. I swear that there were whole families having picnics waiting to see the spectacle (that was my wild imagination).

There was Lenny Aylen - Jaffa - Wild Bill McGraff - Dave Kuti - Dean Haggerty - Mick Biagioni (a bunch of complete maniacs): plus my mate, Dave's younger brother, Eugene and me.

Lenny gave an order.
"In a straight line - side by side."
Eugene and I were walking ahead giving it the biggun.
"For fuck sake! Will you two stop fucking about and get in line"
We did what we were told and marched in line shoulder to shoulder with the rest of them - to our doom.

As we got closer the tension in my stomach was hitting panic level and my heart was pounding. There must have been over a hundred of them. However, the unexpected - what seemed sheer unshaken confidence shook our opponents nerve - we were an unknown quantity messing with their heads - they backed off and parted as we marched on through.

We had called their bluff - and 'finished it'…

"Oh my god, I remember that - a firm from Stratford. Those were the days, no one messed with me, Lenny and Jaffa, in all those years we stood undefeated, I remember being one hundred strong one night in Wanstead. That firm was the birth of the West Ham ICF - Southbank..." (Dave Kuti)

"Fantastic, good old days, them boys from The George pub back then were a proper firm. I remember forty soldiers going to the Heathcote in Leytonstone for a showdown. Nasty stuff: meat hooks, hammers, trowels - won't go into detail. Amazing that you can remember so long ago B. But true enough!!! Great story Barrie. Cheers..." (Paul Wheatley - 'Winkle')

The Sting
In recent years I have lost three people that I felt close to at different stages in my life - today Lascelle informed me that I had lost another friend. Although I had not seen Lazarious Charles for many years my memory immediately ignited.

1974 - I first met Laz the way I met most of my friends - through music. I was in a kid's home near Upton Park - I am not sure if Laz lived in the home or nearby (uncharacteristically my memory has not stored that snippet of info) but he hung out there with a little crew of very cool and stylish older black boys. They were always laughing - joking - singing - dancing.

As always I had my treasured cassette player with me. This bit I remember well - I was on the street sitting on a wall listening over and over again to the JBs 'More Peas'. "Why the fuck do you listen to that wog music!"

OUTSIDE THE LINES

*My Original 7"
Record - I Stuck
White Circles
On My Records
Depicting That
They Were Mine*

I looked up and there were two rockabillies staring at me with deep hate embedded in their eyes. I did not reply, I just stared back. Even though I knew it was not going to end well I was not in the least bit worried. One boy stepped forward and grabbed my cassette player - I was not going to let go but I knew I was about to lose it: they were much older and bigger than me. "Let the fuckin' thing go!"

Laz was not too tall yet built like a prize-fighter: wide shoulders and tiny waist. "You wanna call me a wog?" The boy let go of my cassette player and they both quickly scurried off.

"Thank you" - I was relieved.

Memoirs Of A Naughty Boy #2

1978 - Laz - Anita Hudson & Tiffany

OUTSIDE THE LINES

"Nah man no need - I like wog music" - we smiled.

I next saw Laz on the following Friday night at the Lively Lady in Leytonstone. The club was packed - the room was thick with smoke and the heavy music consumed the dancers within its rhythm. No ventilation - we were all soaked to the skin with sweat. The record that we all had been waiting for came on - 'The Sting' by Barry Waite: it was new and almost impossible to buy (although I had already secured a copy from Moondogs).

There was what looked like a disturbance in the middle of the dance floor - when I got closer it was Curtis and Francis tussling each other to dance with Laz. Up until recently guys would Hustle with their girlfriends - 'The Hustle' was a bit like jiving yet subtler with much more style and finesse. As funk music got looser and heavier young men were no longer dancing with girls - they were dancing together: getting down - freaking out - competing.

Laz and a few of his friends had created their own style of Hustle. Two guys dancing together - power and energy. Hands gripped tight so that they could literally throw each other to the full length of their extended arms - then drag each other back to spin around together and repeat the gymnastics in the opposite direction. Very much in the style of the Jitterbug or Lindy hop - which I recognised from the 1940s movie Hellzapoppin that I had recently seen on the TV.

Laz and Francis were tearing up the floor with the whole club watching. I had never seen anything like it - it was like viewing an old movie. They were dressed in 1930s style - beige loose/tapered pants, white canvas naval officer shoes and white shirts - Laz with his processed hair greased back. Lazarious was king of the dance floor...

Maxie Wanted To Be White
1975 - Maxie was tall - pretty - intelligent - kind - polite: but she hated being black.

I had not seen Maxie for at least three years: she had changed - she did not smile - she had cut her Afro long hair and brushed it almost straight - her face was raw from 'scrubbing off the black' with bleach - she wore white powdery theatrical pancake to hide the darkness of her skin (although not particularly dark). She wandered around the grounds of Doctor Barnardo's silently like a ghost.

I remembered Maxie as bubbly and light - dancing and singing - not a care in the world. I enjoyed her energy and her soft nature - she was always nice to me: she shared her sweets. Maxie was lovely until she started secondary school. She was hated - bullied - teased - taunted - beaten with a stick - called a 'Nappy Headed Nigga'.

She believed that being black was a curse - a sin - that the world hated her for her blackness. She became a victim of her innocence and the hardness of the world.

I saw Maxie one last time in 1977 on the westbound platform of Redbridge tube station. She also saw me - we recognised each other - there was no exchange: as usual no words would fit my mouth.

This is the first time I have ever shared these thoughts - today something that jogged my memory...

OUTSIDE THE LINES

Theresa Tomms
Until I was 9 yers old David Bailey (no not that David Bailey) was my best junior school friend - that was until he called me a 'Brownie' and I beat the crap out of him. I had just come back from Australia and my skin was a very dark tan. It was not that I understood the connotations of what he had called me - it was the way he spat out his parents' hateful rhetoric with such venom.

Once when David and me were playing on scaffolding below one of the bridges that crossed the River Roding he stood on the end of a scaffolding plank which upended and tipped him almost into the river. He managed to cling onto a scaffolding pole - I struggled to drag him up again by the waistband of his trousers. His feet were dangling in the fast flowing freezing water: neither of us could swim.

Next door to David lived Theresa Tomms who also attended the same junior school. She was tall - pretty - athletic - confident - outspoken - tough - the fastest under 12s sprinter in the district. I became strange friends with Theresa. Strange as in she challenged, ridiculed and laughed at me as often as she could: even started the odd fight with me. Despite that we were friends and often had a lot of fun together playing in the street and getting up to my favourite thing - mischief.

After junior school I only saw her upon the odd occasion, we would hang out a few times, then not see each other for a while, she was quite wild and elusive with a lot of stuff/drama going on in her life: a troubled soul.

Summer 1975 - One afternoon I came across her sunbathing at Valentines Park Lido - I always went there alone; my friends seemed to have very different interests.

1968 - My Birthday - (Left To Right) Spencer Stern, Michael Chips, Me, David Perl, Kevin Walbank & *David Bailey*

"Wotcha."
"Wotcha loser, whatya up ta?"
"Nuffin."
She looked amazing - all grown up - swept back long wheat coloured hair - long muscular legs - flat stomached - petite firm breasts: she felt my stare.
"Whatya lookin' at? Nuthin' new 'ere!"
"I've never seen you here before and never looking like that."
"Like what?"
"Like that!"
I was wearing Speedos and my erection apparent.
"What's that? You've grown."
Laughing at me - I was sooOOOooo embarrassed.

OUTSIDE THE LINES

1969 - Redbridge Junior School Class Photo - Theresa Tomms Back Row 3rd From Right - Me 3rd Row 6th From Right: Totally Distracted From the Present

"Sit down silly - I'm rolling a joint." I immediately sat down - hot and uneasy - I could feel my heart heavily pounding in my chest. "Don't worry, I have that effect on men - well, in your case, boy." Again she laughed at me. She got out a packet of weed, rolled a number and we got stoned under the hot sun.

We lay next to each other engulfed in sun's warmth - daydreaming.
Out of nowhere - "I bet you would like to fuck me!"
I was immediately aroused - "Yeah."
"I have a small room in Ilford - let's go back there."
We went back to her bedsit in Ilford and fucked.

I stayed the night with Theresa - we did not talk much. In the morning she was snorting a line of white powder. I did not know much about that kind of stuff and assumed cocaine.

Memoirs Of A Naughty Boy #2

1975 - Valentines Park Lido

"Want a line?"
"What is it?"
"Sulphate - speed, it will pick you up and make you fly!"
"Okay." I snorted a line and flew - this would become my new vice.

As I got into the swing of sulphate I discovered blues - small blue pills that gave almost immediate gratification. Cheap and more convenient: easier to obtain than sulphate. The first half hour of blues brought extreme elation - I desired to talk and be friendly with everyone - of course I did not talk and was not friendly with anyone: I kept it all in my head. When that feeling wore off I was hyper-energetic - six hours later I was moody, irritable and felt aggressive.

OUTSIDE THE LINES

This became a daily cycle. Nightime in bed was hell - no sleep - tossing and turning - cold sweats: cocooned in thought.

Eventually, circa 1978, speed caught up with me. During the day I did six hours of ballet - night-time I went to the Dance Centre, on Floral Street in Covent Garden, to do a few contemporary dance classes followed by dancing in a club until the early hours: repeating the same routine the next day. Besides mood swings and no sleep the other downside of blues is lack of appetite - I would go a whole day on a few apples, Kit Kats and Lucozade: I lost much weight. I became weak and ended up sleeping all day at my parents' house. My mum eventually called the doctor in - I had glandular fever - I spent the next three months in bed.

Sometime in that period I heard that Theresa Tomms had died from a drug overdose...

I Thought You Might Have Been A Bender
Late 1975 - I was kind of on remand in Pentonville - long story (told in full in the previous book: being in an adults prison at 15 years old is pivotal to the story). I spent most of my time in my cell - I wanted out as soon as possible and did not want to attract unwanted attention nor trouble from other inmates.

I read a lot, exercised and stretched: keeping my mind and body supple. At mealtimes I would leave the confines of my cage - hence had to mix with the other inmates: most of them much older than me.

I ate on a table with 5 other prisoners. One, who seemed only a bit older than me, was bright and talkative - built like a brick shithouse. He always seemed to know what he was talking about: often he would look over at me as I listened and gave a crooked grin. He never spoke to me though - I thought he might have been a nine bob note.

One evening I came out to eat - they were all there and the bright one was chatting away. I had not eaten since the previous lunchtime thusly no one had seen me for a day and a half
"Where you been?"
"Minding my own business."
They all laughed. I ate and left.

The next morning I thought I would have some porridge. He was sitting at the table on his own - it was a bit late and no one else was around.
"What's your game then?"
I was puzzled.
"You spend all day in your cell and speak to no one. You're a cocky little cunt even though you don't say nuffin: too defiant for your own good mate. I'm surprised that either the screws ain't done you over or one of the older gentlemen in here ain't had you shivved - so what is with you?"
I was actually a bit surprised - none of this had occurred to me.
"It's my old man I guess."
"Why - is he connected?"
"Nah - he's the connection."
We both laughed.

I spoke up. "I thought you might have been a bender."
"You cocky cunt! You dance around your cell like a fucking fairy. I gotta say though you ain't flash like the most of the kids I meet in nick - I ain't seen you trying to prove yourself or poncing fags at every given chance."
"What have I got to be flash about? I got caught, now I'm in 'ere."

OUTSIDE THE LINES

We became friends and spoke often. He was quite a notorious armed bank robber - the only problem was he kept getting apprehended. In later years he turned his life around and became a successful author.

He was due to appear before the beak in a few days and decided to leave me with a some words of wisdom. "You don't say much but you're smart - smarter than the rest of these cunts - I've watched the way you manoeuvre around different people - you know how to deal with everyone in a different way; no one in 'ere knows where they stand with you. Yeah you are a smart little cunt and you called me a bender."
We laughed.
"You shouldn't be 'ere - this life ain't for you. Yeah, you're tuff and don't show that you give a shit but you've got another side to you - different from anyone I've met. Hope they don't go heavy on your sentence - you need to be out of this shithole". Fortunately I listened - I knew he was right - I never saw him again.

Words of my father:
5) The man who is in prison got caught.
9) If you are going to risk imprisonment - be sure it's worth it…

In The Closet
1976 - Many of my stories seem to be bizarre to others - this particular story is bizarre to me.

We were wandering around St. James' - Maxine Cirillo and I - the girl who first took me to the Lacy Lady (in my first book). I guess she was my girlfriend - or, at the time, the girl I was having regular sex with: she had an insatiable appetite.

Looking for opportunities to obtain profit through petty crime we wandered into mansion-block offices in Ormond Yard. It was 8pm on a sweltering Friday evening and the building seemed empty.

Maxine was wearing very few clothes - short skirt - white vest - white Converse - no bra - no knickers: she was a little minx and most distracting for my immature 16-year-old mind - I kept touching her.
She laughed - "Stop it!"
I couldn't help myself.

We ignored the reception area, went up the marble staircase to the first floor and into the first huge wood panelled office. Whilst I was rifling the drawers Maxine plonked her sweaty fit body on a huge leather Chesterfield, pulled up her skirt and touched herself.
"Look!"
Although aroused - "Have you gone fucking mad?"
"I'm hot."
"Me too but I'm not playing with my fucking cock am I!"
She laughed at my discomfort.

Next floor - nothing much there either except a couple of good pens: a gold Parker and a Mont Blanc - straight in my pocket. Here she slumped into a swivelling leather executive chair, spread her legs and placed her feet on the oak desk - skirt hitched up to her waist. I was struggling - aroused and nervous - we were breaking and entering for fuck sake.

"Come and lick me."
"No - fuck off!"

Next floor - for what seemed like a posh solicitor's office there were very few spoils to be had. I felt we should leave - it was all a bit too easy. "C'mon let's go."

We headed for the stairs but froze upon hearing the voices of people coming up - three maybe four different male voices. My mind was working overtime - they had come back from a meeting - the pub - a meal: not that it mattered - we were in the poo.

"Quick up 'ere." We ran up the fourth floor - the top floor - no more floors - we were trapped. Maxine opened a door - it was a decent sized closet of sorts. Laughing - "In here." - she was not taking this at all seriously.

In the closet I pulled the door closed and listened. It seemed only one pair of shoes climbing to the top floor - clip~clip / clip~clip; the sound of metal quarter-tips on the marble staircase.

The closet was pitch black - fortunately very cool compared to the temperature of the offices. I listened intensely - he sat in a creaky chair - poured a drink - opened drawers - shuffled papers - poured another drink. I pictured a young man in a navy chalk-striped suit - crisp white shirt - club tie - shiny black toe-capped Oxfords. Of course this was all in my head: it could have been some old tramp for all I knew. I thought/think too much.

My ear to the door - the same repeated noises - creaky chair - pouring a drink - opened drawers - shuffled papers - pouring another drink. It seemed like an age yet probably no more than twenty minutes.

What was she doing behind me? My focus re-directed from what was going on outside to what was going on inside. I could hear her rustling about in the darkness - Oh No! - I could literally hear her fingering herself. Clearly she had lost the plot.

"Come here." She whispered - "Come and play with me."
"Shush - no."

She pulled my arm hard - I almost stumbled. I was next to her - the smell of sweat and sex was unnerving - I guess I did not smell great either - I was drenched in sweat and the closet was now warming up. I gave in and played with her breasts - licked her nipples. Literally, from her mouth, she let out a squeak - with my hand I managed to cover Maxine's lips almost suffocating her: of course she fucking liked that. Her hand was straight down the front of my pants.

After much intense exploration - with surprisingly little noise - we came to an exhausted standstill. I went back to the door - silence - the man seemed to have gone or had he heard us and gone for help? Nah - I doubted it.

I opened the door - lights off and office empty - the stair lights were also switched off. Halfway down the stairs we came across a fire exit. I did not fancy taking the risk of leaving through the front: besides I presumed it was now locked. I pushed the metal bars of the exit door and the fucking alarm went off - Whoo~Whoo fucking Whoo~Whoo.

I literally dragged Maxine through the doors and down the flimsy metal fire escape into the warm muggy night. The whole time she giggled…

OUTSIDE THE LINES

I Had To Stab Him
1977 - A year of many firsts for me. My first motorbike - I discovered cannabis oil - lived with a girl - my first stabbing.

My motorbike was a Honda 400/4 - pretty tasty in its day. I rode it like a muppet: had I been killed I would have deserved it. However, this is not relevant to this story.

The discovery of cannabis oil was a revelation - not only did it space me out but could also be smoked by merely spreading on the outside of a cigarette (I hated cigarettes - but hey). Perfect for someone who struggled with rolling joints. Again this does not have any relevance to the following story.

The summer was fading and the nights drawing in - I was living just off the Fulham Road with a junior hair stylist at Vidal Sassoon. I met Nancy at The Room At The Top - she was a punk from Rainham. Five feet ten inches - slim - androgynous - very pretty - jet-black cropped hair with tufts sticking up either side sculpted into cat's ears. Although a punk her clothes were bought from the expensive boutiques on South Molton Street.

We got on fine and of course I loved living on Fulham Road - quite upmarket for an East End boy. She paid the rent (I had no income) - did all the food shopping - cooking etc. I listened to music - smoked cannabis oil - took LSD - had sex with her at every given opportunity. At night we would go to local bars and the odd club. We had very different musical tastes - she was into New Wave and me, never faltering, loved listening and dancing to funk: no middle ground.

Our only real issue was neither of us spoke much. I actually knew very little about her and guess I also did not give much away either. I was used to other

1970s - The Chelsea Drug Store - Now McDonalds

people talking and me listening. Both of us being incapable of casual banter was becoming boring. I liked others to talk - I was interested in people's stories and listened hoping to learn something new.

One cold wet evening I met her from work - Vidal Sassoon on Brook Street - we took a bus to The Chelsea Drug Store on King's Road: trendy in the 60s and early 70s but now shabby and dated. It was almost empty except for a few poncey businessmen in their pinstriped suits and shiny black shoes. We sat in the corner, her with vodka and lime and me with an orange juice. Silence - I was becoming quite agitated. "If you don't talk we may as well go home". I of course blamed her for our lack of exchange.

We left: the rain was now quite heavy so we walked fast. As we crossed the

OUTSIDE THE LINES

King's Road, to cut through a side street leading onto the Fulham Road, two Teddy boys stepped out in front of us. The rivalry between Teddy boys and punks was the latest news - doing battle along the King's Road amongst Saturday afternoon shoppers. I was not a punk and did not dress as one - Nancy on the other hand, although not really a Punk, did dress as one and had the crowning hairstyle to match.

"Where ya goin'?"
'Silence' - they stepped closer - I could smell stale beer and cigarettes: our lack of response gave them courage.
"Where ya fuckin' goin' - PUNKS?"

I heard the click - a flick knife had been activated: I cannot say that I was not scared because I probably was. The problem was that I had no idea which one had the knife and I did not wish to wait to find out the inconvenient way. I stepped back almost forgetting about Nancy; quickly I grabbed her and dragged her behind me. "Run" - she ran - I did not join her. I could now see them clearly, I was calm and took in the whole picture as I scanned them from head to toe.

The taller of the two had the blade. They were smartly dressed (not to my taste). Identical navy-blue drape jackets - silly tight drainpipe jeans - white shirts with black lace ties - blue suede brothel creepers: all quite clichéd. I kicked him in the bollocks (his knees buckled) and head-butted his mate - breaking his nose (fuck was I lucky) - not what they were expecting. I took the knife and stabbed the tall one in the ribs and ran after Nancy.

"What happened?"
"Nothing."
"You have blood on your cuff!"

"Nothing!"
Nancy and I split up a few weeks later.

Now that I think about it I am not sure if this is one story or two stories rolled into one which involved two different girls and a trip to Southend. Both involved Teds and Punks and both ended with a similar result…

Smack On Sundays
1979 - for no rhyme nor reason on Sundays we started jacking up heroin.

Names, times and places in this story have been changed for those whom would be mortified if exposed for their youthful sins.

We would meet at Howard's parents' huge elaborate house in Hampstead - his dad had done well for himself on the stock market. Howard had his own private area at the top of the house - with en-suite bathroom. There were usually three or four of us, but only Howard and I jacked up - the others snorted, smoked or chased the dragon: I always had to go one stage further. Howard always scored the best hence a tad too much may have killed us.

I don't actually know how we got into it - the first few times we threw up so what compelled us to continue?

I would sit calmly whilst my blood supply was cut off with a tourniquet. I watched the lemon water and heroin concoction heated in a spoon by a lighter held underneath the spoons bowl. The bubbling brown fluid then sucked into the syringe through a cigarette filter and any air bubbles tapped out. A suitable protruding vein was located and then the needle penetrated my flesh. I was actually petrified of injections. The plunger was pushed and the fluid released

OUTSIDE THE LINES

into my awaiting body.

The loosening of the arm strap allowed the blood to race through my veins - sweeping up the heroin and depositing it into my brain. The rush was similar to the launching of Apollo 13 - then the soothing release into a soft world of dreams. I could understand the addiction to this heavenly experience: no more worries - pain - anxiety - stress.

I remember one occasion as the smack hit me the tiles of the bathroom spun like the rollers on a one-armed bandit - slowing down for the jackpot as heroin seeped into my senses.

I think the reason I eventually stopped was the painful inability to pee whilst high. Yeah - no one ever talks about the inconvenience of not being able to pee on heroin…!

In The Sand
For personal and legal reasons dates, exact events and places cannot be mentioned.

I have seen enough to know that I have seen too much.

It was long ago yet still I dream of this tragic moment in time. My transition from a boy to a man: although I may not have been mentally equipped for the task.

The daytime desert sun was of 120°F blistering heat. To avoid the searing heat upon my skin my body was wrapped from head to toe in white muslin.

Memoirs Of A Naughty Boy #2

As night fell I lay motionless buried in the sand - breathing the hot air through a short reed: my breath shallow. I was alone - scared - silent - still.

I heard the screams of women and children. The smoke from burning tyres made me gag. I could not make a sound - that could have resulted in my death.

OUTSIDE THE LINES

They were looking for us - I was not the only one buried in the desert. Lonely and petrified - we were three. We knew what must be done if discovered: we had a choice - suicide or bloodshed.

I rose from my shallow grave - sand flying - sweat from my brow burning my eyes - my keffiyeh flaying in the night breeze.

The stinging sweat obscured my vision - the dark of the night limited my view. I turned towards the burning tyres - I saw their silhouettes: I saw their brutality.

My companions too rose from their shallow desert graves, full of confusion and fear: the burning rubber choking them.

Four people would die that night. Our youth lost and our souls scarred forever in time. Now all of my brothers have tragically passed. Still I remain to dream…

The Specials
1980 - 'I just Can't Stand It' - sleeping whilst listening to The Specials new album (More Specials) on my Walkman - I woke up startled when I heard: "Good night Terry - good night Rhoda" - I thought someone was in my room.

Skip forward to 1989 - at a party in Paul Weller's house:
"Hi I'm Rhoda." I instinctively recognised the voice.
"What - 'good night Terry - good night Rhoda'- that Rhoda?"
As I was leaving
"Goodnight Rhoda."
"Goodnight Barrie."

According to Rhoda: "You stepped back in the room and gave me the strangest of looks."

1984 - Jerry Dammers, the instigator of the Specials, opened the eyes of millions (including mine) to the plight of Nelson Mandela with his new band Special AKA and the record 'Free Nelson Mandela'. One man's music - heard by many...

The Crab Claw Necklace
1981 - Cannes - it was 8am and already the sun like a reassuring warm hug was beating down on the back of my neck.

Walking through the hustling bustling market square savouring a warm oven fresh baguette as if it was the best meal I had ever experienced. I had returned a crate of beer bottles to get back the 5 centimes deposit per bottle - enough to buy me a freshly baked warm baguette. No butter - no culinary content: just the stick of bread - a veritable delight.

I nodded to those I was familiar with - exchanged the odd smile - "Bonjour" (sans exchange of pleasantries - I did not speak the language very well) "Comment ça va?" It was a good carefree morning for a young man who was living his life in the South of France.

There was always the odd confrontation on the street - raised voices - arguments - scuffles - usually I paid no mind. Today just off the road I noticed an acquaintance - an old Algerian dude: as far as I knew he was once a revered ships captain in the French Navy. Now a dignified down and out adorned in his button 4 - show 4 - double breasted naval blazer - brass buttons dulled. Three well-dressed Frenchmen were hassling Ibrahim: usually a mild-mannered man

OUTSIDE THE LINES

August 2019

1981 - Port Grimaud -
Wearing Said Crab Claw Necklace.

he seemed agitated by his hasslers.

Ibrahim was speaking fast in what sounded like broken French - whilst the well-dressed gents laughed as if sharing a familiar joke. I perceived that they were trying to bully Ibrahim out of his treasured crab claw necklace. He always wore the crab claws - as a young cabin boy he had made himself the pendent. He clearly did not want to sell and tightened his fist securely around the trinket. I wandered over and watched inquisitively. The three men became aggressive - voices were raised - one grabbed Ibrahim's bicep.

Oh fuck it - "Vas te faire foutre!"
"Que veux-tu?"
I had no idea what was said to me - my grasp of French was poor.
"VAS TE FAIRE FOUTRE!"

All three turned to me and decided to take my advice: they 'fucked off'. Ibrahim took me in his arms, hugged me close and with a tear in his eye spoke in Algerian. He then carefully took off his necklace and placed it over my head and around my neck. He turned and walked away - I never saw him again.

A passerby translated what Ibrahim has said to me - "If you ever gift the necklace to another there will be forever a curse upon your head."

To this day I treasure Ibrahim's crab claw necklace…

On The French Riviera
1981 - The Casino de Monte Carlo was built in 1850 - the most elaborate and fashionable of the Monaco casinos. I was the guest of a glorious middle-aged Argentinian millionaire whom had me hanging around - 'merely for the thrill of me' (whatever that meant).

(Backstory) - I was a dancer at La Playa Club in Frejus - dancing for tips: I was both popular and prosperous. Araceli Attias had taken a shine to me - she wanted me as her toy. She made a financial offer to the club owner that he did not want to refuse - he sacked me and she bought me - in return I lived in luxury accommodation, ate like a king and had plenty of pocket money.

The actual casino socialising bored me but the pretence of the lifestyle - glitz - glamour - money aroused and stimulated my young and impressionable mind; a fantasy of what could be. I was often in the company of great artists, writers, musicians, actors, photographers - Warren Beatty, Robert Mapplethorpe, Harold Robbins, David Bowie, Grace Jones. There were many others whose names I now forget - to be honest I had no idea who many of them were in the first place.

OUTSIDE THE LINES

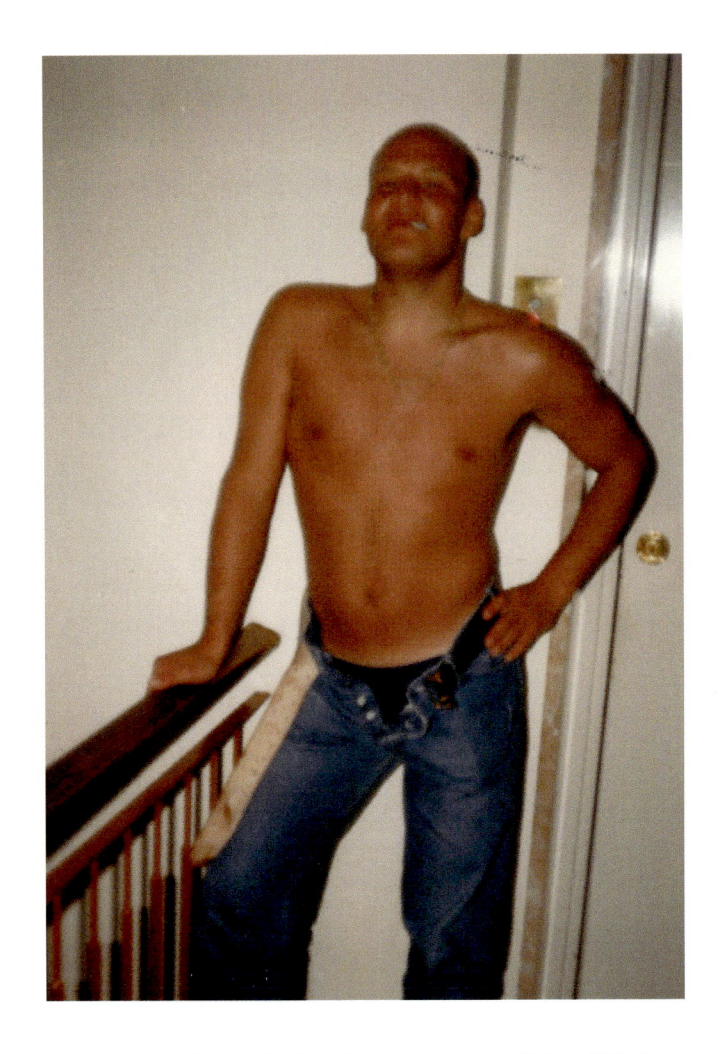

She was not always nice and often berated me in public - "Oh he may look pretty but he is only good for spending my money and accepting gifts - quite useless really." But hey, what could I say? She was right. I actually hated the poncey clothes she bought for me: preferring Levis 501s - Palladium khaki canvas legionnaire boots - simple T-shirt.

I often received expensive watches: she would never notice their absence after I sold them on the street. For a short period this is how I survived and quite happy to do so.

One specific night I was to meet my new 'benefactors'.

We left the casino in Araceli's Alfa Romeo (boat-tail) Spider. She drove along the coast, roof down with the smell of the sea and warm salty air in my face. We were on the way to a gathering where all the 'hip people' were to congregate.

We arrived at a secluded mansion set back off the beach, the décor 70s tacky, the main room set up as a disco with the appropriate music playing. The guests in their slinky - shiny - loud - disco outfits danced around in gay abandon: not a care in their privileged world.

There was nothing actually there for me: middle-aged people drinking expensive cocktails, smoking fat cigars and snorting cocaine off of a girl's belly or off of a young man's erect penis. Crazy shit was going down but I proceeded about my business - what went on was not my concern - I preferred it so.

Although as rule I did not drink, I did upon occasion partake in tequila, LSD and on this particular evening I also indulged in some coke - not really my thing but I was offered and considered it best not to offend.

Due to the combination of poisons I was losing my sense of reality and was struggling to focus on the now. This was not the place to lose it - I trusted none of them - especially in a state of psychedelic obscurity.

OUTSIDE THE LINES

I took a walk in the garden to clear my head and managed to hold it together for the rest of the party. It was almost over, guests were slowly departing, the music turned down and I was hoping to leave soon.

I was sitting silently in the corner upon a velvet throne, quite enjoying the surrealism of my environment: hundreds of miles away from home in a mansion with loads of people who had more wealth than I could ever possibly imagine. I was alone and vulnerable: totally comfortable in this risk-taking situation. Besides, I could actually look after myself and would have had no qualms about using my knife if needs be. Yes, I always carried a knife - I did not trust these rich foreign fuckers.

Almost - yet not quite over.

A beautiful woman approached me, I perceived early 30s, followed closely behind by a huge bull-like man - way beyond her years - looking like he had been in many gruelling boxing matches: I thought him to be her bodyguard. He stood back whilst she stroked my cheek with one hand and ran the other up my thigh, straying to my crotch: I was uncomfortable yet aroused.

"Glorious". She was Italian, yet with only a soft accent. "You see that ugly man, he's my husband, he desires for you to fuck me - it is also my desire. It is your choice - but say no and he will have you disappear."

Clearly an offer I could not refuse - of course I should have - but I didn't. I was an opportunist - an edge walker. I was at my best when functioning upon adrenalin.

There were some minor complications: my Argentinian friend was far from happy - actually quite aggressive, with the threat that I would have to leave

Monaco: which was fine because I was leaving for Cannes.

In Cannes I was to stay with my new friends in their lush chateau - a short ride out of town. The décor understated Deco - the serene surrounding land was vast - the gated entrance guarded by smart suited men.

I knew all was not as it seemed; obviously the bull-like man was either a high-powered businessman or a gangster. It turned out that he was the latter: he was some kind of mafia boss. He wanted to be present whilst I pleasured his wife. He clearly did not like me and was often abusive in Italian. He spoke no English - though I was sure he knew what I was saying hence not liberal with my words.

He was at least six feet two inches - huge shoulders with a thick trunk. His head seemed oversized and his features, ears, nose, etcetera exaggerated. He had a shock of thick greying brown hair, neatly groomed and always wore one of his many conservative tailored suits. His immaculately polished bespoke black shoes were a size thirteen. His face battered and scarred. In all to look at a very scary man - almost giantesque. His persona reeked of violence: a fuck I did not give - the immediate situation worked for me.

Besides him not liking me all seemed well - two weeks later I was still there. I had my own private area with en suite shower room. I was more or less left to my own devices, just as long as his wife was pleasured: as was he - in his own personal way.

I rarely left the chateau. The man was often away on business and the lady busied herself either in the beautiful gardens or indulged herself in me. I sometimes went with her shopping for lush flowing dresses and skirts which she liked to wear on all occasions - more importantly her husband liked them.

OUTSIDE THE LINES

I quite enjoyed the shopping trips: happy to tag along and give my approval.

One overcast drizzly morning - "Cheri, I am going shopping for a few hours. Would you like to come along? Armando will be home sometime today and I want to look nice for him - he expects something special tonight."
"Nah - it's cold and I am worn out - I need to sleep."
I went back to bed and drifted off.

'Crash'!
Someone was throwing stuff around in the living room. I heard him shouting - "Stronzo" - I knew the curse was directed at me.

Oh fuck it - the old cunt. I put on my boxers and went to face him. Shit: he was purple with rage. Launching himself at me he wrapped his arm around my neck from behind - his forearm crushing my windpipe: fuck I was dying.

I bent my knees and pushed upwards throwing us both against the bar - he let loose his grip. Whilst gasping for breath I grabbed the ice pick from the ice bowl - I was going to stab him in the eye or temple: the old cunt.

I was almost focused and ready to attack. She came in grinning - the grin twisted into a distorted scream - then a stream of fast Italian abuse. They got into a heated verbal exchange: I thought he was going to throttle her. The voices softened - she had managed to calm him. I had no idea what it was all about but it was time for my departure.

The lady spoke soft and fast. "Get all your stuff and be ready to leave in five minutes you are no longer welcome here. I will have the driver drop you at the train station - get on a train and leave: today!"

"Are you sure that your driver is not going to take me on a short trip?" I mused. She laughed nervously. "You have been watching too many gangster movies - if that was the case you would already be dead"...

Antiques Dealer To Duffer
1982 - My parents' neighbours were an old German couple - Jewish refugees that had fled the 1940s horrors of Nazi Germany. I had left home many years before thus had little to do with them. They did not much like me - nor I them.

Heinz Stern was a short stout man who always wore a grey 1940s heavyweight Loden wool suit with a grey fedora perched upon his head. His wife Zeta was a woman of small stature that wore a matching grey skirt suit, also with a tiny Austrian style hiking fedora. Both of them Bavarian in style.

The Sterns had no family to speak of and lived quite solitary lives: usually up at the crack of dawn for a brisk walk. Mid 1982 they both died within months of each other: first him then her. The house was left empty - no one laid claim to it. The house may have been empty of people but was full of antiques.

Although I did not live at my parent's home I had the front door key so that I could sneak in during the daytime (when no one was about) to take a shower and use the washing machine. Everytime I visited I looked through the windows of the Stern house to try to figure what exactly was in there.

One afternoon I thought 'fuck it I'm going in' and that is exactly what I did. Over the back fence and forced my way through the French doors with ease. The place was full of old stuff: lamps - ornaments - china - paintings - jewellery - ancient hi-fi - antique clothing. What was I gonna do with all this stuff? More importantly how was I gonna transport it? I could not use the front door

OUTSIDE THE LINES

1984 - My One & Only Certificate

hence to conceal my crime I had to make several journeys: out the back - over the fence - through my parent's garage.

Over three weeks and many journeys I cleared the whole house: I stored the stuff in my East Ham flat. Right - I had to clear all of this old toot. My girlfriend at the time, Diana Brown, came up with the solution - Portobello Road Antiques Market. I enquired and was informed that I would have to turn up on Friday/Saturday mornings at 4am, queue up and hopefully I could secure a pitch.

The Toby (rent collector or in this case the market inspector) did his dealing from an orange VW Camper Van. A short rotund character with a pathetic curly perm. I really did not like this man - he was a slag, going out of his way to be obnoxious to show me that he was the boss. Had I not needed his assistance I would have fucked him right off. I kept my mouth shut and head down, which boded very badly with me.

I would turn up, pitch out and stand in the freezing cold until punters started to arrive. I had some good stuff and I displayed it well. After a while I got the hang of it and was most successful: the only issue was that my stock was diminishing. I had a few bob so early in the mornings I started checking out the Golborne Road bric-a-brac market, from there I purchased cheap yet attractive items that I could sell on my own stall with a more than healthy profit margin. There were plenty of things to buy - I specialised in chrome artefacts and wooden writing boxes - I even started restoring the boxes which ended up with me attending the London College of Furniture where I became the best in my class at French Polishing. That all came to an end when I started hanging out with a group of stylish dudes who would eventually (with me) become the 'Duffers' (of St. George)…

My Cousin's Ferrari
I mentioned in my previous book that I was residing in a shared house - one of the occupants being my crazy cousin Samual I wrote that 'there is another story' - here is the story.

1982 - Samual - a nice middle-class Jewish boy from a well-to-do family on my mother's side - living in Chigwell (k'nuckas). He had done very well for himself with his bespoke curtain and furnishings business.

Apart from being a nice well suited and booted Jewish boy - Samual had a vicious and violent streak; short-tempered and ready to kick off at any excuse. I was once present whilst he beat the crap out of his 'Jewish princess' girlfriend.

OUTSIDE THE LINES

I was either too immature or too stupid to stop him - I certainly should have: one of my many failures.

Samual had gotten himself banned from driving - probably for his accumulation of speeding convictions: he was an adrenaline freak. For a substantial fee I became his designated full-time driver - his car being a red 1970s Ferrari (Targa top) with custom-made royal blue suede seats. I have no idea of the model - flash cars were never my thing. What I do know is that the heavy clutch pressure pained my knee.

Samual's clients were rich Arabs mainly residing in Mayfair. For measuring up and fitting to requirement he would have the keys to their empty apartments - I too had access to these keys. Often I would spend the night in these flats - sometimes houses or mansions: either alone or with a female friend. I certainly looked the part driving my loud Ferrari. Of course the odd Rolex watch, Dunhill lighter and Mont Blanc - Parker - Papermate pen found its way into my pocket.

One sunny afternoon driving Samual along the North Circular to Golders Green - Targa roof removed - a police Panda car started following us. The lone policeman had done his research via two-way radio and obviously concluded that the owner of this speeding vehicle was on a driving ban.

He sounded his siren, flashed his beacon and pulled us over. I stopped, wound down my window and waited for him to trod over.

"Yes officer?"
"Which one of you was driving?" He stupidly asked.
I was a bit miffed - however always having a snappy answer pointed to Samual from my place in the driver's seat - "He is".

"Oh, you think you're funny do you? Out of the car the pair of you". I got out. "Well, you did ask a stupid question." He got out his notebook. "I will show you who's stupid!"

Uh Oh - Samual was now out of the car. "Right you cunt - fuck off before I come round there and kick the shit out of you!" The officer, no older than us (early 20s), was mortified and appeared to be scared. "Yeah, best listen to my friend or we will kick the shit out of you - now fuck off!" '

'Fuck off' he did - back into his little Panda and off along the North Circ.

Boomerangs
In 1968 we lived in Australia - I did all the standard Australian things - surfed - played with kangaroos - threw my boomerang - but it never ever came back.

1983 - I came across said boomerang in my parents' garage. I went straight to the park and threw it hard into the air. It soared like a bird, only to come crashing down onto the tarmac footpath and broke. Clearly not built for an urban environment.

Upon inspection I realised that the solid piece of Australian Blackwood was heavy and brittle. I challenged myself to make a lighter more flexible version.

In the garage I set up a jigsaw on the workbench and sourced an electric sander. I studied the broken boomerang - it was intricately shaped and asymmetrical at either end. There was clearly sorcery instilled into the making of this weapon.

I spent hours in the British Library sifting through relevant books until I came across one written in big words with lots of pictures and diagrams: no boring

OUTSIDE THE LINES

Crafted By My Own Fair Hand

long-winded wordy details. Having found that which I sought I slipped the book under my coat and off home to study (not at any time have I suggested that I was nice).

Right - so boomerangs are left and right hand specific, depending on how one finely hones the contours during construction. A fifty thousand-year-old tradition - not specifically of Australian origin - originally carved from animal bone. Left and right indeed: a stupid concept!

I decided to construct from aircraft ply - produced from layers of thinly cut mahogany bonded together to achieve malleability with no excess weight.

First I hand-sculpted a template - after several attempts achieving perfection: due to OCD perfection being essential. I then whittled to shape, electronically sanded and finished with fine hand sanding to master the aerodynamic contours for flight. Once manipulated to satisfaction I soaked overnight in linseed oil -

concluding with a thin coat of yacht varnish.

It flew - it flew well - yet never came back: I could not master the trajectory of the winds in the open fields.

There I was happily producing boomerangs (I shit you not). I even convinced a local car sales showroom to purchase a hundred as a promotional tool with their logo on the front - stencilled on the back - 'You Always Come Back To Anthony Cope'. Happy, that was until my concentration waned. I felt a hot stinging sensation in my left middle finger which was placed under the wood as I cut. I jumped back and looked at the gap at the top of my finger; it then turned red with blood.

I wrapped the wound with a cloth, jumped into my Mini and sped off to King George's casualty for three stitches - I still bear the scar…

Pretty Poison
1983 - My crazy cousin Samual appropriated an idea off of a friend of his - Debra Yudolph. She came up with the concept 'Pretty Poison': sending dead flowers to people whom you do not like. I created a flyer using Letraset and we were in business.

Dressed as a chauffeur - I was the delivery boy. Somehow the project managed to gain momentum and the next thing I knew all three of us were invited for a live interview on ITV's 'Bill Grundy Show'.

When arriving at the ITV studio we were shown to our seats in the audience. Samual and I were placed in the front row, Debra was seated elsewhere towards the back - they had made up their minds that she would not be a part of their

Produced By My Own Fair Hand - Stuarts Phone Number

story: extremely unfair considering that it was originally her concept and not ours. At that age I was not articulate enough to protest the injustice.

After the break the camera panned towards Samual, he explained 'his' idea and how 'he' came up with the concept.

The camera was then pointed at me. "Barrie I understand that you have had some weird and wacky encounters on your deliveries." (The voice of Bill

Grundy).

Not a great speaker at the best of times, but in public - on TV - I was mortified. "Well yeah, on Valentine's day I had to deliver to a couple of women who had jilted their boyfriends. The first threw them in my face - the second poured a bucket of water on me from the third-floor balcony as I left the building. On other occasions men have threatened and been abusive towards me - women have sworn at me - one spat at me and another invited me in." (I did not mention having sex with the one that invited me in).

Due to Samual's betrayal the drive home was in silence. I felt for Debra: however, I had no way of articulating it.

Recent conversation - *"Barrie that's so sweet. In my youth I had a terrible Inferiority complex and that experience was just reinforcement to me that everyone was better, cooler, prettier, thinner than me! I was terrified of you and always thought you hated me or just didn't know I existed. So stupid I know but now I know you realised how bad I felt. Paula Yates was one of the hosts and she was flirting with Samual..."* (Debra Yudolph)

Margaret Thatcher
The Thatcher generation, my generation, was the last generation to have a broad and varied education: social and worldly as well as academic. We had strong role models - we were taught right from wrong - we knew the difference. At the time I was politically unaware of the irreparable damage being caused by Thatcher.

(My perception in short) - Thatcher gave the rebellious intelligent working class a chance to buy their own homes that in reality they could not afford

OUTSIDE THE LINES

- 'better themselves'. The repayment of these mortgages was above their pay-grade. Low interest rates soon increased - the prices of houses fell leaving many new homeowners in negative equity. The formally 'rebellious intelligent working class', whom now deemed themselves 'middle class', went in fear of losing their homes and newly found social status were now silenced...

Whispers Wine Bar
1983 - I first met Brenda at Whispers Wine Bar on the Romford Road in Manor Park. On Sunday nights funky music was played by a dude I knew named Linz. Brenda, who worked at Whispers, had her eye on me. Later that year myself, Eddie, Marco and Cliff (pre-Duffer days) put on a party further down from Whispers just behind the Romford Road at The Uppercut Club on Earlham Grove. This would have been right at the beginning of my record-playing career, I may have played once or twice before. I played once at the Titanic in a sound clash with Sean Oliver and Neneh Cherry against the resident DJs and also at Poufy Dave's birthday party in Chigwell with Derek B - I am not sure in which order.

We called the party 'Xibaba (She-Ba-Ba) Pa Ti'. It was the first time I had DJ'd with Lascelle (thirty eight years later we are still playing together). The Uppercut Club was previously a boxing gym and now available to hire out for functions. For a small sum we secured a Saturday night and invited all our friends and local dancers. All the best dancers lived in the East End - well maybe not the best - however, many of the good dancers came from the East End.

Whilst I was DJ'ing Brenda and her two sisters were dancing about smiling at me whilst whispering and giggling. Melba was the one that spoke to me, she told me that her younger sister Brenda really liked me, but I asked about

Flyer Designed By Marco Cairns (Duffer)

the older sister - it turned out that Lena had a boyfriend so I ended up seeing Brenda.

I was never that serious about Brenda but she was always hanging around at my flat - also on Romford Road. What I remember most was her always wearing my clothes and her continuous demand for sex - I guess this stopped any desire on my part for other women.

One warm summer evening I bumped into Linz - who lived just around the corner - he was struggling to carry two large speakers on his shoulders so I gave him a hand in taking the speakers to his yard. It turned out that Linz was owed money by the Whispers management and had taken the speakers as compensation - I did not know this at the time, although it would not have made much difference if I had.

I was reasonably friendly with Cheri the Cypriot woman whose husband Jim owned Whispers and her younger sister. The Duffer boys and I would often go in there on the quiet weekday evenings for a camp piña colada and chat to the sisters.

Early one evening Brenda came round to my flat and to tell me that Cheri and Jim wanted to talk to me. I got dressed and ambled down to the bar for a chat. Cheri was waiting behind the well-stocked plush bar backed by huge mirrors.

"Rumour has it that you stole a pair of speakers from us."
"Well I didn't."
"You know who did though - don't you?"
"No."
"We know you had something to do with it."
"No you don't."
"Brenda told us it was you!"

I knew this was a lie. One thing I hate is injustice - somebody accusing me of something that I did not do is the one thing guaranteed to provoke a reaction. Without any thought process, and to be honest before considering or knowing what I was doing, I launched a huge ashtray at the mirror behind her, shattering the glass and smashing many of the exotic liqueur bottles. I turned and calmly left. I literally lived three minutes up the road; when I got home I had that familiar 'what the fuck have I just done' discussion with myself.

Chaotic: people were called in and interrogated by Cheri and her husband - even Brenda's mum. Much to my relief, even though I resided so close, they could not find out where I lived - no one was willing to grass. Apparently 'the Cypriot Mafia wanted to pay me a visit': empty threats always amused me. My only mild concern was getting nicked for something stupid when I was actually innocent in the first place.

My relationship with Brenda ended in the summer of 1984 - something to do with her older sister - whatever it was now escapes me…

Rene Gelston

I have not always had it easy - often not made it easy for myself yet I do not feel that I had it hard, yes my mother was mentally ill for most of my life and often I was in social care but I never went hungry - I played, had fun and except by choice always had a roof over my head. One thing is for sure no one ever gave me anything. I had to work for - fight for - take what I wanted - no one presented it to me except for one man: Rene Gelston.

In 1984 Rene gave me my one and only break: he invited me to DJ at his new weekly event - 'Black Market' at the Wag Club - this opened many doors. Although naïve, and at 24 years old had only ever had one honest job, I seized the moment and ran with it. This was only the beginning.

My path was clear - I managed to embrace the many situations that I fell into. I, along with Lascelle Gordon, instigated what was to become the Rare Groove scene. We were both in the band that marked the sound of what was to become Acid Jazz. At the same time I was one of the four creators of Duffer - we shook up the fashion industry worldwide. In my own small way I was a part of the change that took place in fashion, music, club and youth culture.

Being the DJ at possibly (at that time) the world's trendiest nightclub, playing to London's elite, I was noticed. The DJ box was on a rostrum slightly above the dance floor - hence what I was wearing was seen and noted. What I was wearing could also be purchased at the Duffer store (Portobello Road) on Saturday afternoons. When I wore my Baker-boy cap backwards, my leather Luftwaffe jacket or my Levi's 501s cropped - people wanted to follow suit. When I wore Gucci loafers (sans socks), Gucci loafers became the fashion.

OUTSIDE THE LINES

Rene

It was not that I did anything first, I was influenced by my surroundings and contemporaries - I was not alone; it was where I did it. It was Rene who enabled me to successfully fall uphill...

1984 - Black Market (Wag)

Keeping It Moving

I have previously told the stories of me DJ'ing at The Wag Club: I won't go into it again because the 'Rare Groove' discussion and the bullshit and false claims that go with it I now find tedious. If you were there you already know - if you were not I doubt that you actually care. There is one story I purposely omitted - having confessed my injustice to the said parties I can now share.

Summer 1984 - Rene's Black Market had become the trendiest club night in the world and the platform for Lascelle and I to lay the foundations for what was to become the Rare Groove scene (which you already know). Basically we played our favourite 1970s funk records (and some new ones) in retrospect to a brand new audience, many who had never heard such music before. There was no real masterplan.

OUTSIDE THE LINES

*1984 - Lascelle Lascelles
- Black Market (Wag)*

August 1985 - We gave Rene four weeks notice that we were leaving. We were opening our own club in Leicester Square along with the rest of the Duffer crew - 'The Cat In The Hat'. Rene asked me to recommend some DJs to replace us.

Six months earlier I had DJ'd at Crazy Larry's off the King's Road - a popular yet poncey nightclub. The dude I was playing with was a part-time DJ that played the music of the time - 'Solid Soul', which I could not stand, with a few of the 70s records that Lascelle and I had made popular thrown in.

Steve and I got talking and he explained that he was a courier and wished to get into DJ'ing - he went on to tell me that his older brother had quite a big 70s collection of funk records. Asking if I knew of any gigs he gave me his phone number.

1985 - The Wag - Derek B - Rene Gelston - Horace Carter Allen - Billy McIntosh - Steve Jervier

I gave Steve's number to Rene - recommending him as one of the best DJs I knew. I also recommended my best mate Horace for the job - knowing his record collection at the time was not huge. I was sabotaging the competition. In the long run both were to prove me wrong - Horace Carter-Allen and Steve Jervier became London's premiere DJ's. Indeed, Steve became one of the main importers of Rare Groove and went on with Rene to open Black Market Records - London's premiere house music record store.

Lascelle and I moved on fast and created the band 'Diana Brown & The Brothers' (the foundation for the 'Acid Jazz' sound) - which split into The Brand New Heavies - The Young Disciples - Diana Brown & Barrie K Sharpe...

OUTSIDE THE LINES

Slim Gaillard - The Wag - 1984 - Shot by Dave Swindells

Slim Gaillard

Every Friday night a tall grey haired old man would turn up at Black Market. Bespoke suits - hand painted kipper ties - polished well-heeled shoes - white beret: quite popular with the young ladies.

One night as the club was emptying he was hovering about and proceeded over to where I was packing my records away. "Hey man (in a regal American accent) the music you dude's play is sweet - the best DJs I have ever heard. The way you two tell a story with the records takes me on a journey. Solid!" ('Two' = Lascelle and I).

The next Duffer warehouse party we put on (Clink Street - Borough Market) he was there with two lady friend, standing all night close to the decks rocking to the rhythm and drinking from a silver flask: "Solid man - Solid."

Everywhere we played he was there. Everyone seemed to know him - his name was Slim Gaillard - which meant absolutely nothing to me - nevertheless he was really cool.

A one-sided conversation at the Cat In The Hat club. "Hey man that was a great set - you dudes (Lascelle and I) have such a flow with this music - I never knows where you are going to take me." I thanked him and explained we grew up with this music - it was a main feature in our lives. "Man, just keep on doing it, you bring joy into this old man's life - I thank you for that."

Bulee 'Slim' Gaillard (1911 - 1991) - creator of his own jazz vocalese, 'Vout' - rose to prominence in the late 1930s with hit record 'Flat Foot Floogie'. In the 1940s played and performed with the greats of Be-Bop - such as Charlie Parker and Dizzy Gillespie. Also notably playing a cameo roll in Hellzapoppin'.

Slim's daughter (Janis Hunter) became Marvin Gaye's second wife (Jan Gaye) - the singer/actress Nona Gaye being his granddaughter…

Dance Shoot With Ray Petri
1986 - Friday night - The Cat In The Hat - Ray Petri approached me: "Hey Barrie - I've been watching you dance. I love the way you move - so graceful - as if you are weightless - I'd love to do a shoot with you moving like that."

Ray Petri was 'Buffalo'. There were a few of them in the agency but Ray was recognised as the stylist and his name carried weight. Before Ray and Buffalo 'stylists' were not a thing. Buffalo made styling into a business that became integral to the fashion industry and press. Buffalo was also integral to the commercial success of Duffer.

Now - I knew Ray was gay and I knew he liked masculine young men hence I

OUTSIDE THE LINES

suspected his possible intentions.

"What'ya gonna do with the images?"
"They are just for me - for the art of it - because we can."
Me being me - "Yeah when?"

We did the shoot on that Sunday afternoon in a little studio just off of Ladbroke Grove. I am 99% sure that my mate Mac took the photos.

Attired in the latest Duffer style I did my thing to James Brown's 'Papa Don't Take No Mess'. I got deep into it - contorting and twisting my body within the rhythm. For me dancing was a religious experience - I was lost in my element, getting down for the whole self-indulgent fourteen minutes of the track.

Mac happily snapped away. Ray was clearly getting off on the whole spectacle. All I wanted out of it was the photos - from which I created a collage…

Royal

1989 - For many years - on and off - I studied and practised Wing Chun with various teachers. Throughout this training I often heard the name Sid Sofos mentioned - to many he is an iconic master.

February '89 - we (at Duffer) opened a very exclusive club - 'Royal' - in a plush hostess club situated in Mayfair.

From the get-go the management was difficult to deal with regarding their door policy and dress code. Duffer was the pinnacle of fashion yet Sid the doorman vetted whether people could, or could not, come in merely by judging their attire and trusting his own taste.

As one can imagine this was the cause of many confrontations.

One warm summer evening I was called to the door because Sid would not let in Diana Brown's Italian boyfriend - I arrived at the door to see Sid blocking his entrance. Nino was wearing shorts and canvas sneakers and Sid was having none of it. I went upstairs to speak to the manager - (who possessed the best teeth numbing cocaine that I had ever experienced).

"Yeah - don't worry I'll come down and sort it out." When we got to the front door the manager looked at Nino and had a change of heart.

"No - he is not coming in!"
Sid winked at me - I was not happy.
"OK - wait!"
And off I went.

Zaki Dee was DJ'ing. I hurriedly packed my records away and told Zak to do

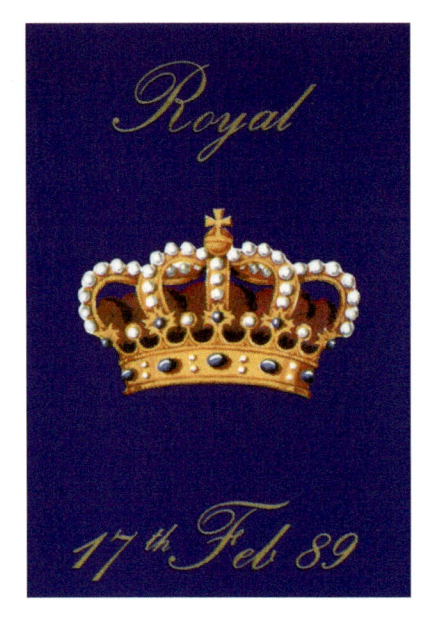

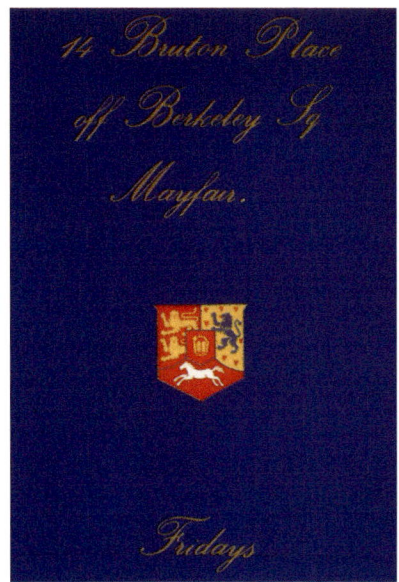

Flyer Designed by Marco Cairns (Duffer)

the same. When we were ready - the last record (which was playing) was put in Zak's box - we left via the side entrance.

There I was outside the front door standing right in front of Sid and smiling - record box in hand: he soon realised that there was no music playing. I casually turned and left.

Apparently the management had to resort to putting on the radio.

A year later - Great Marlborough Street Magistrates Court - I was waiting with Eddie and Marco to be to be called as a witness for an altercation that took place in the Duffer store between Eddie and the police - which I had actually instigated by antagonising a policeman who was trying to give me a parking ticket - he eventually decided to arrest me - I ran through the store and out the back fire escape into the night. Meanwhile Eddie was tackled to the floor by six constables and arrested.

Lo and behold - Sid was also waiting in the foyer to be called as a witness for a different case.

"Ello boys how's it going?"
We shook hands and exchanged pleasantries.
"I gotta say I always had a lot of respect for you boys."
Before any of us could reply he was called into the court.
"Sid Sofos - you are required in Court No.1"

The penny dropped - Sid was legendry 'Sid Sofos'…

The Marchioness Tragedy
Saturday August 20th 1989 - a photography agent's birthday party. London's beautiful people - models - photographers - journalists - designers - artists - fashion editors.

I was waiting for a phone call from Horace - Horace was waiting for a call from Neville - thankfully the call never came. My wife Hiywet and I stayed home that night. We never saw Neville again.

Fifty-one people lost their lives that night on the Marchioness - quite a few of whom I knew...

OUTSIDE THE LINES

Roy Ayers
One of the notable episodes of my life was snorting cocaine off a toilet seat with Roy Ayers when our paths crossed on tour. As a young man in the early 1970s to me he was a revolutionary musical icon.

1991 - I met Roy Ayers at a Sunday afternoon gathering at Gilles Peterson's house. At the time I had a record in the UK and American charts and was introduced to Roy as 'the producer of Masterplan' - a tune that he was familiar with: $$$ signs registered in his eyes. I guess he mistakenly confused me for a successful record producer and songwriter rather than the hustler that I really was - merely stumbling uphill.

We hit it off and spent the whole afternoon chatting about music - specifically his early 70s music career which fascinated me. Unfortunately I found him to be on the hustle - seeing the smaller image rather than the big picture. "We can do this - we can do that." Not realising that I had actually very little to offer.

We met again a year later at the Prestatyn Jazz Weekender. I was there with my mates from the band Galliano who happened to be performing on the same bill as Roy. I was going to play tambourine with the band - merely because I was there.

Roy saw me. "Hey Barrie my man - how you doin' son?" Again I felt a disingenuous hustle - he still thought that I was something that I was not. We hugged (most uncomfortable) and shared some small talk. He shook hands with my friends - Constantine and Rob Galliano. Roy was on Rob immediately ($$$).

Rob - "Would you do us the honour of coming on stage and performing a

song with the band?"
Roy - "Yes of course!"
Roy wandered off to his dressing room.

I spoke up - "He ain't coming on any stage with no Galliano."
Constantine - "Whad'ya mean? Of course he is - why are you are being so negative man?"
Rob gave me a funny look - no more was said.

The gig was going great - Galliano is one of the best live bands I have ever seen - the crowd was in a frenzy.

"Ladies, gentlemen - I now have the pleasure of introducing to you one of the musical greats who is going to honour us with his presence on stage."

No one came - no Roy Ayers - there was a short pause and then the show continued - sans Mr Ayers. I continued playing the tambourine: smiling bad-mindedly to myself.

"How did you know B?" Rob asked.
"How much money did you offer him? Did you think that he had flown all the way from America to join Galliano on stage in a Welsh holiday camp without you paying him!"

A recent exchange with Rob. "I announced Roy Ayers and there was dead air time."

A few years ago Rob told me that back in the day I had shared a Sharpism with him: 'In life you may open many doors - unfortunately you will not be entering them all'...

OUTSIDE THE LINES

Malawi
This particular story is a bit obscure and has some vividly blurred lines - it took me quite a while to creatively piece it together.

1992 - I do not know exactly why but I became good friends with the son of a very well known and successful (1960s/70s) stand up comedian who had worked his way up from the seedy back street northern comedy clubs to stardom at the London Palladium.

He was an odd well-spoken middle-class fellow with some serious issues - by the time this came to light it was too late - for this reason I shall only refer to him as 'Tea'.

A while earlier Tea had split up with Sally - his childhood sweetheart. He was devastated and had this wild notion that backpacking across Africa would be the cure that would get him over her. He flew to North Africa and indeed started his epic trek across the continent. The stories of his experiences were amazing - jungles - gorillas - giant waterfalls - torrential rain - much walking.

For reasons which I cannot to this day explain I met up with him in Malawi. We located ourselves in a hut by the magnificent lake - as huge as an ocean. There was very little to do but swim, smoke Malawi Gold and drop LSD; which I just happened to have had handy. Tea was very funny (with his public schoolboy humour), we had many laughs and shared much jovial banter.

The sun was a constant swelter of life-giving heat - it felt good on the body - though by midday it was treacherous. We decided upon a trip to the uninhabited small island that we had been observing for quite a while in the distance of the lake. It just seemed like a good idea at the time.

We arranged for one of the local villagers to row us out there. A young guy named Sampson was eager to take us - merely to converse in English, which he had been studying. He spoke my native tongue very well, probably better than me, yet he struggled with the speed of my cockney accent - as did/do many.

The boat was basic - ten foot long - wooden slats - two wooden bench seats - one set of oars: not particularly exotic. The journey took circa forty minutes - nothing exciting besides us tripping out of our heads on acid - Tea and me, not Sampson - he was totally oblivious of our heightened psychedelic mental state.

We disembarked, found a satisfactory seating spot in the shade of a Mpingo tree (source of African Blackwood - the wood of boomerangs) and stared out to sea. Not many words were exchanged; Sampson made himself busy around the boat - Tea and I continued to sit and stare and hallucinate.

Tea spoke:
"What do you mean?"
I re-tuned to reality and looked at him - his distorted face was glowing red and his eyes wild.
"I didn't say anything."
"You did - what do you mean?"
I ignored him - I was on my own little trip.
Again - "What do you mean? You're with them aren't you?"
"With who?"
"Them, you know who they are!"
He stood and pointed at Sampson.
"And him, he's with them too! You both are."

Sampson wisely made himself scarce - moving to another part of the island. Tea went silent - once again all was calm. He stood suddenly, gazing long out

OUTSIDE THE LINES

1991 - Malawi - LSD

to sea.

"She's out there on the boat."
"What boat?"
"You can see it - you weren't going tell me; she has been on that boat all along!"

He was having a bad trip and I in no fit state to deal with it.

Shit - he was making his way to the rowboat: what the hell was I meant to do? He climbed into the boat and was muttering. "I'm coming Sally - I'm coming - wait there - just wait there."

Now I was worried - not for him - if he took the boat how were Sampson (nowhere to be seen) and I meant to get back? Fortunately he stumbled around unable to secure the oars into their locks: quite a spectacle.

I managed to straighten up and shout at him in an extremely officious tone. "Stop! Right fucking now! You're tripping - none of this is real. There is no fucking boat out there and no fucking Sally!!!"

Tea stopped and gazed back out to sea: fortunately he saw no vessels. He slumped into the boat and cried.

"She was there on the boat I swear she was there."
"Yeah - but she wasn't."

All was now tranquil and Sampson returned and rowed us back to safety. I swore to Tea that I would never repeat this story to a soul.

This tale is yet not over.

OUTSIDE THE LINES

Three months after my return home I became very ill. Hiywet (my wife) got me to the doctor who claimed that I had flu. "No I do not have flu - I have been to Malawi and I am very fucking ill!"

I continued to be ill.

Tea called Hiywet and explained that he had recently returned and was now also very ill. Luckily his father arranged an appointment with a tropical disease specialist - we both had contracted Schistosomiasis.

The doc casually explained. "This is a simple problem to solve. I will give you both a course of three pills to be taken with two-day intervals. You will either be cured within a few weeks - if not - you might die within five years."

Schistosomiasis, also known as bilharzia, is a disease caused by parasitic flatworms called schistosomes: which can survive in the body for up to thirty years. The urinary tract or the intestines may be infected. Symptoms include abdominal pain, diarrhoea, bloody stool, or blood in the urine and possible death...

Daleks
31 October 1993 - My wife Hiywet was pregnant and our baby almost due. It was a Saturday night, not much going on in the baby stakes, so I went out with Horace to do some dancing at Bar Circa in Grosvenor Square. I had just purchased one of those new mobile phone gadgets - a huge contraption: rather inconvenient for a night of dancing. I still have the same phone number today. 4am - as we were leaving I checked my phone - I had a missed call so immediately called home. Hiywet's friend Sarah answered in a panic. "She has just gone into labour".

Westminster Bridge - Licensed From Flash News

I calmed her down and asked questions; I had read up on this stuff and been to all the antenatal classes. No need to panic there was still a way to go. I rushed home to Clapham in about fifteen minutes. I assessed the situation and decided it was time to take Hiywet to the hospital. At St. Thomas' we had to wait around in the waiting room - still a bit early.

OUTSIDE THE LINES

I kept Hiywet calm by massaging her back and shoulders - she was prone to panic attacks and this was not the time for an episode. I am not sure how I ascertained, but it was time. I called the nurse and indeed she was in labour - we proceeded to the delivery room.

7am - whilst Hiywet was in labour with my son Manassah I was gazing across Westminster Bridge towards Big Ben. Seven Daleks appeared to be coming across the bridge - no people around - just Daleks.

"Look - Daleks!"

No one looked - no one listened - no one cared - I merely attracted a few bemused glances. I had not taken LSD the previous evening (to this day my drug of choice) hence I suspected that I was actually looking at Daleks.

The Dalek experience often came to mind: today I researched and indeed - 31st October 1993 eight Daleks crossed Westminster Bridge…

Opium
Apparently there are a lot of rumours regarding this story - one I heard recently of me killing my best friend whilst we were on holiday - here are the cold facts.

1995 - My wife Hiywet and I had split and my eighteen-month-old son Manassah resided with me: at this time Hiywet was living and working in NYC. To make this work I had left Duffer and with Japanese backing created Sharpeye in Japan.

Running my new clothing design company and dedicating myself to my son meant I could only work from 10am to 3pm. There were no child-minders

1995 - Goa

in this equation, or any other outside help. I was rebelling against my own upbringing - 100% hands-on and attentive. I shaped my life around my son's needs. All this was taking its toll.

My son's mother returned to London to see him - it was decided that Manassah should go back with her to NYC for a short while until I would eventually go and collect him. For me this was a welcome and much-needed break. With a sense of weightlessness I boarded a plane bound for Goa in search of dreams.

Upon arriving at Goa International Airport I bumped into a guy who knew me from Portobello Road market, he was travelling with his French/Algerian boyfriend - Jabra: a fashion stylist that also seemed to know me. They gave me some advice, where to go, where to stay etc. My path with Jabra would soon

OUTSIDE THE LINES

cross again.

I spent my days by the pool browning my worn-out body in the hot sun and the evenings wasted on opium: and why not? You only live once and my mind needed rest to clear itself of life's flotsam and jetsam. One evening I was sitting on some steps staring at the stars and along came smiley Jabra. "Hey, I found a source for the baddest opium. Fancy getting high?" I immediately confirmed that I did fancy getting high. Jabra disappeared - yet did not return. After a few hours I was bored and retired to my room.

3am - Bang~Bang~Bang upon my door.
"Hey B wake up."
I reluctantly opened the door and there was Jabra's smiley face.
"I couldn't get the O - but I have something better."
He opened a wrap and showed me the brown powder. I looked him in the eyes.
"You know that shit will kill you!"
"Nah - it's fine."
So we sat and he prepared some lines.
I looked him in the eyes once more
"Are we not going to smoke it - that shit will kill you!"
"Nah - it's fine."
So we both snorted a line of heroin.

I lay in the bed feeling like crap - nodding in and out of reality - not enjoying. Jabra was nodding in a chair smiling contently. Through a shimmering haze I could hear Jabra talking to me.

"More?"
"NO! That shit will kill you."
"Nah - it's fine."

I dozed off - waking to run to the toilet to puke up - I was not in a good way. I lay back down realising Jabra was moaning in a very low tone: I was too out of it to give a shit.

I woke suddenly at 6am - the sun shining through the open window was burning into my eyes. I could hear it - I had heard of it - I had read about it: 'The Death Rattle'. A low rasping sound from deep in the back of the throat of a person overdosed on drugs. I was too far-gone to care.

I woke again at 9am (a habit of always checking the time) - I looked at Jabra - no smile - I knew he was dead.

'The Death Rattle - end stage wet respirations occur when secretions build up in the throat and airway'.

A few months later Jabra's brother made contact - requesting to come and see me. I was obliging. A few hours prior to his arrival (he had flown from Paris) I was getting a bit worried - was he going to be distraught or angry - he may have blamed me for his brother's death and want to try kill me?

He was very softly spoken and enquired regarding the circumstances of Jabra's demise. It did not seem that he deemed me to responsible for his brother's unfortunate passing. The Indian police had been vague - they had omitted any suggestion of drug misadventure: that would have been bad for business. I told it as it was - his main concern was his mother finding out that Jabra had died from an overdose. I assured him I had told no one. For reasons of self-preservation all traces of drugs were flushed before the police arrived.

Jabra was not his real name...

OUTSIDE THE LINES

1985 - Original Duffers - Portobello Road - Myself, Cliff Bowen, Eddie Prendergast, Marco Cairns

The Demise Of Duffer

Often I am asked why I was 'sacked' from Duffer - 'Sacked'…?

Being one of the four creators - owners - one of the two designers: be assured - I was not 'sacked'…!

By 1995 Duffer could no longer financially sustain itself: accumulating much debt with suppliers and manufacturers.

I was not involved with the finances - that was Eddie; those who know him can work it out for themselves.

Jeff Banks introduced us to a flash German tennis champion who fancied himself as a fashion entrepreneur. He bought the company for the amount that we were indebted for - not a penny more and not a penny less. He wished for the three partners (what happened to Cliff is another story) to remain and run the business. The moron had not figured out that we were not capable of running the company - hence our financial predicament. I did not like this suntanned 'international playboy' and he did not like me. The plonka wore his sunglasses at night.

In his own words - "I don't understand a single word that Barrie Sharpe says; he talks so fast and with that funny cockney accent of his."

As previously recounted > six months earlier I had secured a deal with a Japanese backer to set up Sharpeye in Japan. I had already planned to leave to care for my son.

Duffer became a world-class multi-million £££ fashion brand - no longer an icon of international style. Had I remained this may not have happened. Eventually JD Sports bought Duffer's accumulated debts and rebranded it as a sports label.

2020 - I remain Sharpeye...

OUTSIDE THE LINES

Sharpeye Backstory

We at Duffer had taken a substantial amount of money from a Japanese fashion house - 'Ready Steady Go' - to produce for them an autumn/winter 95 clothing range. We were in serious financial difficulty hence used the money to pay off some of our many debts.

Of course no one told the Japanese client of our predicament. It came up at a meeting and it was decided that Eddie would have to tell them of the situation - which he did not do: this played into my hands.

Wishing to leave Duffer I came up with a cunning plan. I contacted the English agent for our Ready Steady Go advising the state of play.

We had spunked their money
We had not started to produce their collection
We had no intention of producing a collection for them
However - I proposed
For no fee I would design them a collection
We would call it 'Sharpeye'.

If successful we would negotiate a deal to go forward with Sharpeye in Japan - it was successful thusly we went forward.

I naively asked them to register the Sharpeye trade mark in Japan on my behalf: of course they had already registered the trademark in their name - I said nothing.

For the next six month I accumulated from them as much money as I could - in the meantime devising another cunning plan. I designed and registered a new Japanese trademark - 'Suiceyed'. To the naked eye, of those in the know, when applied to a garment the label appeared to read 'Sharpeye'.

I contacted Ready Steady Go's English agent and informed him that I knew of the Sharpeye trademark deception that Japanese company had perpetuated. "They can go fuck themselves. They may own the Japanese trademark - but they do not own me. Good luck with designing Sharpeye without Sharpeye."

Suiceyed blew up in Japan and I opened a Sharpeye store in London's West Soho - at the time the heart of media land - PR agencies, film and music companies etc. Sharpeye became numero uno amongst fashionistas…

L.A. Connection
1996 - I was staying in the Gramercy Park area of NYC at my estranged wife's sister's luxury high rise apartment, overlooking Manhattan. One of those bijou style gaffs owned by model agencies to accommodate high flying top models (my sister-in-law being one of them). Perfect for me, central and just around the corner from my mate Earle who was residing on Lexington Avenue. A much needed break from bringing up my son: he was hard work - even at three years old a bundle of energy.

OUTSIDE THE LINES

One afternoon - lunching at Stingy Lulu's (where I met Lisa Rudolph - that's another story of drugs - strippers - LSD and a ménage à trois) on the Lower East Side (Alphabet City) - Earle received a business call from Paul Stewart: A&R man at Delicious Vinyl and American manager of the Brand New Heavies.

"Hey Paul - how you doing?"
I could not hear the reply.
"I'm good too - having lunch with Barrie Sharpe."
Apparently Paul replied.
"Barrie K Sharpe! I've been trying to reach him for a while regarding managing his music projects here in the States."

Earle passed me the phone – yadda ~ yadda ~ yadda. That evening I am on the Red-Eye to LAX.

I arrived in L.A. at daybreak and was picked up by Paul who drove me in his convertible Mustang (sans roof) - the sun was beating down - to a luxury poolside apartment owned by Delicious Vinyl: this was where I would be staying.

"I'm gonna go see Dr Dre in an hour. Grab a shower and I'll swing by and pick you up: then brunch?" Interesting - the whole time I was in New York all people were talking about was the music of Dr Dre - I on the other hand had never heard of him.

We pulled up to a studio complex in South Central: an area that I only knew from the movies. From the outside the studio looked like a fortress - the inside was lush with state of the art equipment.

Paul indicated for me to sit in the huge games room: video games - pool table - bar - etc. There were three guys in there playing pool. I sat and minded my own business. The tallest of the three came over. "Brer: that hat - what's it about son?" I was donning a white Cuban X-Giants baseball cap with a large red X emblem on the front.

'The Cuban X-Giants was a baseball team in the Negro League - formed at the end of the 1800s - a founding member of the National Association of Coloured Baseball Clubs of the United States and Cuba - disbanding in 1906'.

I explained who the Cuban X-Giants were and where on Harlem's West 125th Street the cap could be acquired.

What intrigued me about this dude was his slight feline stature and the smoothness of the cool slow drawl in his voice - indeed he would make a great rapper.

"Hey Snoop - Dre wants you." (This went over my head - I had never heard of 'Snoop Dogg').

Aggressive vocabulary projected from the studio. Three/four raised voices in a heated argument flying back and forth with venomous speed. After 5 minutes or so Snoop stormed out. As he left the studio his two compadres fell in step and the three departed the building.

The exchange in the studio was now calmer: three voices. Paul came out. "Hey B - come meet Dre." I walked into the huge plush studio - I was transfixed by the AK47 casually leaning against the wall and the odd handgun innocently lying around.

OUTSIDE THE LINES

"Hey."
"Hi."

The third dude approached me. "Hey - I'm Nate - 'Nate Dogg' - Snoop's cuzz." (Again over my head).

We all shook hands - friendly banter exchanged - basic small talk. Dr Dre was quiet until he burst out - "I'm gonna have that muthafucka offed. Nate you need to tell your boy - he signs today or things gettin' messy."

I had no idea of the situation - however:
'Offed'
Ak47
Handguns
South Central
I was not impressed - what insanity was I being subjected to?

Eventually we left. Paul took me for brunch but I was not hungry. He spoke of the great plans he had for Delicious Vinyl, his management company and what he could do for me. I was quiet - thinking - had he intended to impress me with his association with Dr Dre? He certainly missed the mark!

He dropped me off at the apartment at midday - arranging to pick me up at 5pm - after he had done what he had to do. I immediately booked a flight back to JFK - had a swim and left for LAX. Any further contact with Paul Stewart was severed.

Had dreamt all of that? I closed my eyes and broke it down. I vividly pictured Snoop coming over and questioning me with that cool slow drawl in his voice. It was at least a year before I realised who 'Snoop Doggy Dog' was...

Memoirs Of A Naughty Boy #2

*1997 -
Manassah
- Paris*

Manassah Choking

1997 - I was showing the latest Sharpeye Spring/Summer range at Tranoi in Paris.

Manassah was aged four. Whilst I was busy speaking to Japanese buyers and doing interviews he was having the time of his life - running around the exhibition hall making friends with all the designers, all of whom were making a huge fuss of him.

I had not seen Manassah for a while; he tended to come back and forth every so often to check in with me. I noticed him out of the corner of my eye looking a bit distressed. Someone had given him a boiled sweet and he was choking. Panicky people were fussing around him. "Appelez une ambulance." Time

OUTSIDE THE LINES

stood still for a microsecond - fuck the fucking ambulance.

I walked over to him - literally pushing people out of the way (strangely enough my dad was there). I looked at my dad and then my choking son. With my left hand I picked Manassah up by the ankle, hung him upside down and banged hard on his back with the palm of my right hand until the sweet was dislodged and expelled from his body. This all took place in slow motion.

Now calm - I took Manassah in my arms and held him tight - tears running down my face.

My dad looked at me proudly. "How did you know how to do that?"
"I didn't."

No recollection of what my dad was doing there or why he was in Paris…

An NYC Story
Circa 1998 - I have no idea why - I was on a plane to NYC with William Hunt the tailor: an unexpected union. Previously when I was at Duffer he had phoned and asked me if he could have tickets for the 5th Circle catwalk show - I made it clear that if he turned up I would beat the crap out of him. He had ripped off one of the Duffer Yardies - a poor copy that would not harm us in any way, shape nor form: it was the principle - a fucking liberty taken.

I am unsure of the reason for our visit but Willie spoke about himself, how successful he was and how much money he was turning over for the whole eight-hour journey.

We stayed at the Waldorf Hotel on Park Avenue - Willie's choice not mine.

1989 - Duffer Yardie

Willie was a close friend of Michael Hilfiger (known as Michael H) - Tommy Hilfiger's adopted brother. As far as I know Tommy found Michael living on the street, he brought him home and the Hilfigers adopted him.

Michael was a designer in his own right and had his own denim range. He also fronted the rock band 'Michael H and the Bashers'.

We hung out with Michael everyday - he was quite a laugh. We could roll up at any club or restaurant and no matter how long the queue doors would immediately open and we were given impeccable service. We were 'the Hilfiger party'.

One night fifteen of us were politely hustled into an extremely exclusive Moroccan/Arabic restaurant on Mercer Street. The interior was done out like

OUTSIDE THE LINES

a Bedouin harem - sand on the floor - huge tents - hookahs.

I was happily chatting away to a couple of people sitting opposite me - a bald slight man and a very pretty blond lady - nothing deep - I remember there was much laughter.

Michael sat down next to me, hooked his arm around my neck and pulled me towards him - he whispered in my ear.

"Do you even know to whom you are talking?"
"No."
"Well - the woman is Cameron Diaz and the man Michael Stipe - REM."
I gave him a blank look.
"You have absolutely no fucking idea what I am talking about do you?"
"No Michael - and care even less."

I liked Michael H - he was a gentleman that understood my vague nonchalant eccentricity…

David Baldwin
In a NYC taxi circa 1998 with my son - I get a phone call.
"Hey, its Melvin - is that Barrie?"
"Melvin who?"
"Melvin Van Peebles - your friend Lisa said you were in town and gave me your number. I am inviting you and your son for ice cream up in Harlem."

(One year later)
It was not until circa 1999 that we first spoke. I was staying in a NYC Soho apartment (whose I cannot recollect). Having the responsibility of my son the

only chance I got for a real break was to leave him in London with his mum and fly to New York every couple of months. There I could free my mind - body - soul.

It was the early days of mobile phones and I did not always carry mine around with me. One evening upon returning from a long day's walk around the back streets of Manhattan I noticed I had a missed call. I would not have known who it was from because I did not know how to store numbers. I called the number back.

"Hello - this is Barrie Sharpe - you called me."
"Yeah - it's David, David Baldwin - we know each other from the London clubs. I was doing a photo shoot with Melvin Van Peebles and he told me you were back in town and gave me your number."
I had no idea whom I was conversing with but managed to style it out.
"Hi - how ya doin'?"
"I'm good - living up in Harlem on 93rd Street - come up and check me out."

He gave me his address and the next day I took a lazy stroll uptown to see him. I walked up to the 3rd floor of the Brownstone - rung the bell and waited. David answered: I did indeed know him. I had seen David Baldwin around in the West End clubs since circa 1979 - Maunkberrys - The Embassy - Legends: he had his own style and was a fair dancer.

We spent the day hanging out and talking. In the evening I suggested we go to 'The Soul Kitchen' at the Supper Club - put on by Frank, a DJ friend of mine. Lysa Cooper (NYC club celeb) gave me the heads up for this regular funky 70s style party.

By the time we got into the club both David and I were flying on LSD.

OUTSIDE THE LINES

1999 - NYC - Shot By David Baldwin

Throughout the night we drank tequila - danced - snorted cocaine - danced - laughed a lot and attracted a few young ladies with our 'cute English accents'. My Cockney lilt was most popular, although due to the speed I spoke no one had a clue what I was on about - the LSD, tequila and coke enhanced my incomprehensibility. This was how David and I more or less spent the next three weeks: flying on acid with a tequila/cocaine chaser.

One stiflingly hot summer's night Karen B Song (my friend Earle Sebastian's assistant) and I hustled our way into seeing Tricky perform on the Lower Eastside. Now that I think about it, I was trying to get us a squeeze from the promoter, who was standing outside, but he was having none of it. Then some dude with a West Country accent comes over. "They're with me." I figured out from the accent, although I did not actually know him at the time, that it was Tricky himself. After the gig Karen and I went to a gathering at a nearby bar. We sat outside looking up at the stars. I was tripping far out into the cosmos explaining stuff to her. On her own admission at the time she could not make head nor tail of what I spoke - she just thought to herself, 'that's just Barrie being a bit out-there on his own'.

Many years later I get a late night phone call. *"B - hey it's me - Karen. I'm in Korea on acid looking up at the stars in the deep blue/black sky: I now know exactly what you were talking about!"*

I had to return to my son, he was missing me and although he was hard work I too was missing him.

A year or so later David returned to London. We spent time hanging out - mainly on the Portobello Road and in Café Girasol on Tavistock Road. When Manassah was growing up we spent most of my free time there. A great place for him to explore and learn about people. He met all kinds - nice - crazy -

1999 – Manassah - Aggressive Skating

drunk - drugged: he learnt to see who was who and how to negotiate them. He was quite spoilt: many people would make a fuss and treat him to drinks, food, sweets and the odd toy. He had very long hair so most thought he was a pretty little girl - which he manipulated to his advantage.

One afternoon Kylie Minogue sat down at our table - holding out her hand.
"Hi - my name is Kylie - I am a friend of Manassah's."
I took her hand.
"Yeah - I know who you are - but how do you know my son?"
"I often chat with him and see you playing with him in the square."

The Girasol was convenient for me. I could sit outside all day and the people I wanted to see or chat with would usually pass by, whilst Manassah spent his time at 'The PlayStation' skate park fearlessly doing his aggressive skating. He had his own mobile phone hence I did not have to go and check up on him every half hour - also he could call me if he needed to.

As time went by I saw less and less of David. He became distant and started to carry himself awkwardly like a Thunderbirds puppet. I thought he was ill - Alzheimer's or something: he sure was not right. Also he was hanging with some dodgy girl who I disliked and distrusted. I heard rumours that David was 'on the pipe'. Upon hearing this I went to see him to talk and see what was occurring.

We spoke of the beauty of crack and its benefits (David spoke I listened). I decided before trying to reason with him I needed to know what I was dealing with.

"Okay - get your pipe out - let's 'ave a go." I was smoking crack for the first time. Although I kind of got the attraction of the immediate rush - the comedown was so quick; for some reason it made me feel quite dirty. I did not like it. Anyway, knowing that I was wasting my time I had my talk with him. After that I saw very little of David, I just did him the odd favour when he requested. A year later he was dead - his lungs collapsed whilst he was in the bath.

"Amazing: your memory is so good. What a walk down memory lane. I remember you, Graham and me going to the movie house to see 'Saving Private Ryan': whilst you were tripping out on acid - with that crazy opening scene. Then we went to the Coffee Shop in Union Square: what a nice summer night it was out on he streets. Those were some sweet times in downtown New York: before it took a turn for the worse. I forgot about David - I always saw him when you were in town..."
(Karen B Song)

OUTSIDE THE LINES

We Were Drowning
Usually at Christmas I travelled with my son - we would catch a Christmas or Boxing Day flight and find accommodation upon arrival. This year I had decided upon Brazil.

2001 - We arrived in Rio on the 26th of December. The airport was empty - not even passport or customs control. We were on the street within twenty minutes - there was one single cab waiting for a fare.

"Ipanema please."
"Where in Ipanema?" The driver spoke good English.
"The beach - a good hotel by the beach."

He took us took to a good hotel on Ipanema beach. The hotel was quite luxurious. I hustled a good tariff and off to our luxurious room overlooking the beach and next to the swimming pool. We travelled lightly - one large army rucksack, mainly with my son's requirements - I only needed two T-shirts, spare boxers and a pair of shorts: after all I was in Brazil.

My days were spent by the pool; Manassah's were spent roaming the hotel looking for mischief and eating burgers and chips. We left the hotel to eat, buy provisions or to go to the beach. Oh - and of course to buy the boy a Brazil football kit.

I do not like the beach, the sand gets everywhere, the sea is dirty and I am not a great swimmer. Manassah, ever the adventurer, loved it. Even with the language barrier he made friends. He always had a new playmate and was also able to engage adults in conversation: which usually ended with them parting with money or a treat.

Memoirs Of A Naughty Boy #2

2001 - Manassah - Rio

I instilled in him that when swimming in the sea to watch the break of the waves and always be on the beach side of the break. Ipanema has a fierce surf and strong current - many are dragged out to sea - only to be fished out by the helicopters with nets that patrolled the beaches.

One particularly sweltering afternoon, whilst uncomfortably sitting on a beach chair on the water's edge, I was watching Manassah play in the sea with some local boys. I looked away for a minute or two - when I returned my gaze he was unknowingly on the wrong side of the waves. Within seconds without any thought process I had him in my grasp. A huge wave came crashing down slamming me to the floor and I lost him. I was pinned to the ground swallowing sea water knowing that he was in the same predicament. I came up and had

OUTSIDE THE LINES

2001 - Rio - Shot By Manassah

him again only to lose him to the next wave. Men were now in the water trying to get a hold of Manassah: none managed to get a firm grip - the relentless waves kept crashing down on them. I waded to his side - he was in my arms and once again we were hit and pinned. I was drowning. For the first time in my life I panicked: adrenaline took away my breath. Had I not panicked I would have either pulled him out further to where the sea was calm or swam with him diagonally across the current to safety - I knew this stuff!

I had him - we clung to each other - tight in my arms - hugged to my chest: we were bombarded by waves but I refused to let go. "Daddy I want to go home! ~ I want to go home!" Slowly - inch by inch I got him back to shore: no matter how many times the waves hit us I was not letting go. This was not going to happen - my son was not going to be a statistic. When we eventually got to the beach the crowd that had gathered applauded. I sent Manassah to thank the men that tried to help us and I knelt and cried. I cried the very same tears whilst writing this...

The Final Protest
15th Feb 2003 - men - women - children - aunts - uncles - grandparents - brothers - sisters all took to the streets: many of whom were first-time protesters. They were protesting against the onslaught of the invasion of a country that our governments knew could not fight back - Iraq. Genocide justified by government and media lies - deception - fraud - greed.

The people had spoken! The turn out of thirty million worldwide could not be ignored. All whom attended shared the elation of such a successful protest - they had surely won - the protest was a success and historically the worlds biggest.

No! The Iraq war was already set in stone. On the 20th of March 2003 the invasion took place - Iraq was bombed. So was the 'Anti War Protest' merely an illusion of success? Our governments sent out the clear message of 'Fuck You'! I perceive that was the protest that broke the back of protests - ending all hope of future meaningful successful objection. We The People lost.

Before the advent of Facebook I was apolitical - I knew nothing of politics or our so-called 'leaders'. Upon reading FB posts I wished to know why we were invading Iraq - I could fathom no tangible reason for such an extreme measure. Who was this evil Tony Blair character?

Cause and effect: create the problem - resolve said problem using extreme measures.

OUTSIDE THE LINES

Which Islamic country invaded the west - overthrew our leaders - bombed the people - destroyed the infrastructure - left a void for extremism to take control (A rhetorical question)...>
Was it Iraq
Was it Libya
Was it Afghanistan
Was it Syria
Was it Iran
None of the above.

We invaded Iraq
Killed Saddam Hussein
Murdered the indigenous people
Destroyed the infrastructure
Raped the natural resources
Leaving devastation in our wake
A void to be filled by the very militants that we armed
The genocide continues today
Why did we invade Iraq - who are the real terrorists...?

Pubs And Football
I do not like pubs - I do not drink - I do not like drunken people.

I do not like football. At the age of 13, on a wet freezing evening, I was the goalkeeper in a five-a-side football match - at great speed the ball hit me square in the face - I never played football again.

In 1974 I stopped going to West Ham when my South Bank contemporaries started getting seriously tooled up for the matches, eventually becoming known

Memoirs Of A Naughty Boy #2

as the ICF. It was all getting a bit too naughty for me. I did not mind a scrap yet I did not want to stripe anyone nor be striped!

2005 - In a Portobello pub with my mate watching an important football match on a big screen. Actually I was not watching the football - I had no interest - an equally uninterested young lady had caught my attention and we were deep in conversation.

I sensed unease - out of the corner of my eye I saw a brief exchange between my friend and two very tall men. Apparently they were sitting in front of the standing watchers but kept getting up when excited: people kept telling them to sit down because they were blocking the view.

OUTSIDE THE LINES

My mate - "Come on dudes we all wanna see the game!"
Heated words were exchanged and the two gents were approaching my mate.
"Look - I really don't want any trouble."
They were getting closer - I stepped forth.
"You ain't listening - he said he does not want any trouble!"

Their attention and approach was shifted to me. With neither a second thought nor hesitation I had kicked one in the bollox and spanked the other in the hoota. Chaos ensued: it turned out that there was about seven of them.

Four backed me through the crowded first-floor bar onto the balcony and trapped me in the corner. Although trapped none could actually get close to me due to my flying fists - arms - elbows - legs - feet and of course biting. One did manage to get through and whispered to me. "I'm gonna throw you over the balcony." This resulted in the breaking of his nose with my forehead.

My mate was struggling with the other three. I saw an opening, grabbed him and dragged him down the stairs to the street, where we proceeded to run. They were soon after us - relentless - there was no shaking them off.

We got to Tavistock Road Square and I stopped - my mate kept running - I intended to stay and fight.

I was soon surrounded and the next thing I know I was in 'Maria's Café' with my friend Lisa: concussed. The ambulance came but I refused to go to the hospital. By this time there was a quite a crowd. The local homeless guys and junkies were vexed and together we went hunting for my assailants - they were not to be found…

Memoirs Of A Naughty Boy #2

Death By Misadventure
This chapter was sparked by a conversation with my son regarding empathy and how I am always reliable no matter the situation. My mother was neither empathetic nor reliable.

2011 - My mother spent her whole life in and out of hospital with manic depression (bipolar). She was never the same person for very long, forever changing personalities either due to the illness or the 'cure' - shock treatment. Electroshock therapy would wipe her memory - sometimes for days - sometimes for months. She rarely returned to exactly the person that I knew. I learned to understand and accept this: my sister for her own personal reasons is unforgiving.

For me:
The past is in the past
It cannot hurt me unless I allow it to
I do not allow
It is not forgotten
It is not hidden away
It is in its rightful place - the past
A part of who I am and the man it makes me today

My mother never held me tightly with love (I do have recollection of my father's hugs though) - due to this I am uncomfortable with affection - sympathy - praise towards myself - yet I am able to empathise, show appreciation and some affection.

As for hugs - hugging was a longwinded bedtime ritual between my son and me, at least until he reached the age of 12 - "I am too big for a kiss and hug." - although at night he would often sneak into my bed.

OUTSIDE THE LINES

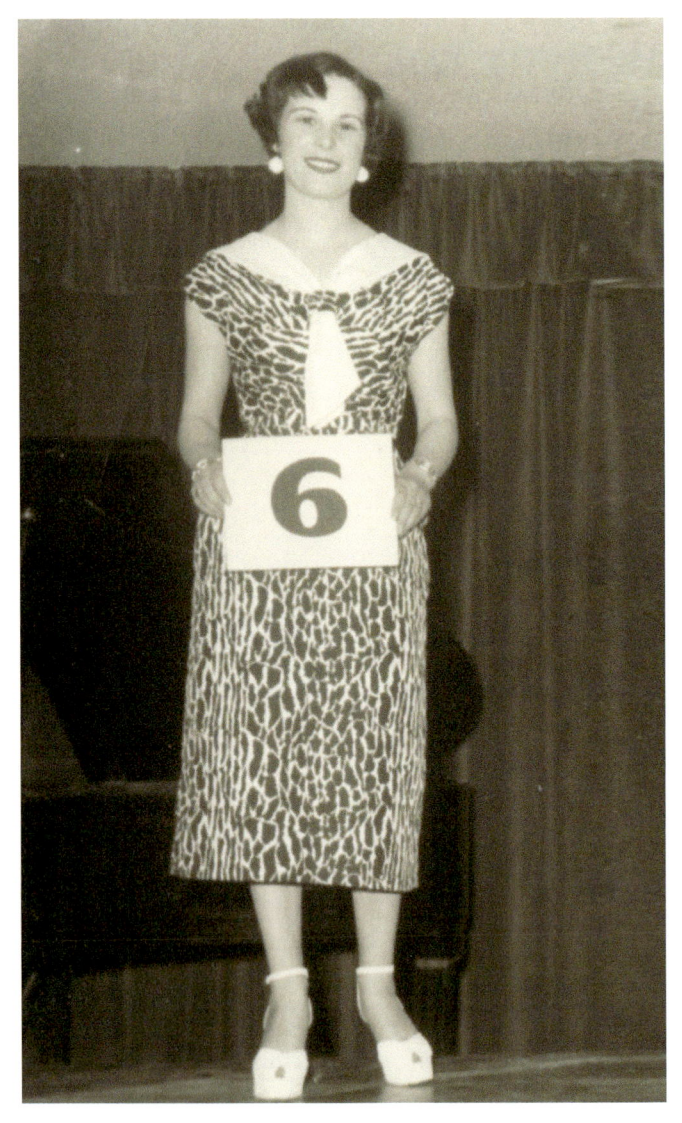

1948 – Sybil Stone – 19 Years Old – Miss Butlins

My home life was a loveless affair - my sister was unkind to me and my mother was often unfaithful to my father - yet for the sake of a stable upbringing for his children he always forgave her. They did not love each other - zero affection. My sister and I could not rely upon my mother for a single thing.

I have one recurring memory of my mum - I would have been no more than 4 years old. My mother had recently returned home from mental care and we were shopping in Ilford's Marks & Spencer. I put on a pair of blue fake leather gloves with a fake fur lining: they were wonderful and I needed them.

"Mummy, Mummy I want these."
"Keep them on then."
We left the store with me wearing my new gloves.
"Excuse me madam, your child has taken a pair of gloves."
"I do not have any children."
A commotion was brewing and straight away a policeman appeared.
"This lady's child has taken a pair of gloves from the store and they have not been paid for!"
"Is this true madam?"
"No! Of course it's not true - that wicked child is not mine."
They took her away and took my sister and I back into the store until my father picked us up.

I did not see my mother again for at least six months: I did not visit her. When she returned she was very different: calm - distant - a stranger that kept calling me 'son'.

I said to my father her attitude had changed (attitude being the wrong word).
"Attitude?"
"She's different."

OUTSIDE THE LINES

1949 - Sybil Stone (My Mum) - 19 Years Old

April 2011 - Goodmayes

Of course she was different. She didn't even know my fucking name!

Following the initial conversation with my son I began addressing the way my mum died: something I may have only ever discussed with one person. Like the rest of my mother's life her passing was just as unconventional - if you knew her it could be considered quite humorous.

On the 5th April I got a call from Goodmayes Mental Health Unit - where my mother resided. "Mr Sharpe, I am sorry to inform you that your mother had an accident last night and is now on a life support system."

With my 8-year-old son (I had no one to look after him at such short notice) I drove down to Goodmayes to be told the grim facts of the situation. I sat my son outside of the registrar's office and went in to hear the details.

OUTSIDE THE LINES

"Last night your mother climbed onto a chair and attempted to tie a noose around her neck, whilst doing so she fell off the chair and broke her arm which caused her to have a heart attack. She is now in a coma and due to a time-lapse of oxygen reaching her brain it's doubtful that she will regain consciousness. Even if she does wake up she will have serious brain deterioration which we doubt that she will recover from. Mr Sharpe as next of kin you have the responsibility to decide whether to prolong the coma via the life support apparatus or face the inevitable and give us permission to switch it off - the latter would be my advice."

Oh the irony - a typical fuck up that only my mother would make.

"Switch it off."
"Okay - it is not immediate she may survive for a few minutes or a few days."
Manassah and I sat by her side in silence for a while.
Softly - "Dad are you okay?"
I stood up, took his hand and we left.

Her passing brought a sense of relief - a burden had lifted.

I have never mourned my mother's death - I do not know how: recently this has been on my mind - I am quite troubled by it.

'Electroconvulsive Therapy (ECT). Formerly known as electroshock therapy. Often referred to as shock treatment, a psychiatric treatment in which seizures are electrically induced in patients to provide relief from mental disorders'...

Incarceration
2011 - My son Manassah was faced with a choice of pleading not guilty to an offence that he did not quite commit - if found guilty he ran the risk of receiving eight years imprisonment, or he could do a deal with the prosecution and plead guilty to a much lesser charge which held a sentence of probation or up to eight months imprisonment. If pleading not guilty he had a 50% chance of walking free; alternatively if found guilty he had a 50% chance of going to prison for something that he did not exactly do.

He was placed in front of a judge fifteen years past retirement age. According to both defence and prosecution barristers he always gave maximum sentence to 'young men of colour'.

I advised my son to plead guilty to the lesser charge. Although he had a chance of beating the unjustified case the risk was too great: he took my advice. Once in court it was clear how ignorant and racist the judge actually was. My son pleaded guilty and was referred for probation and social reports. After an interview and background checks it was recommended that as he had no previous convictions he should not be incarcerated - he did not seem to run the risk of re-offending. A term on probation was advised.

The judge ignored the expert advice and reports.
"I am going to start this trial again - regarding the original charge."
The prosecutor was perturbed.
"That would be unlawful your honour, the defendant has already pleaded guilty to the lesser charge bestowed upon him."
"Don't you tell me what I can and cannot do in my own court!"
"It is the law your honour."
The clerk of the court concurred the prosecutor's fact.

OUTSIDE THE LINES

2011 - Manassah - 18 Years old - After Release *3 Months Later*

"Ah - it says in the police report that the victim was wearing a very expensive pair of Hugo Boss sunglasses - I suspect that this was the reason for the robbery."
"With all due respect your honour the defendant is not on trial for robbery - indeed no robbery was reported."

The judge casually gave my son the maximum sentence allowed of eight months in prison. My son was distraught - I explained:
1. He was lucky - given the chance the judge would have given the full eight years.
2. He should not blame the judge - he alone put himself in a position that gave the system control over his liberty.
3. Although he was not guilty of the original accusation he was not completely innocent on all counts - he was unfortunate to be placed in front of this

particular judge.

After serving three months he was released early from prison on a tag. Three months was long enough to open his eyes to the realities of life. He was on twenty-three hour lock up: plenty of time for him to think. I actually think it did him some good. He came out more respectful - reasonable - humble - appreciating that he is more fortunate than some of the kids who were happy to be incarcerated just to have food and shelter.

For the majority of kids imprisonment does great harm, as they have no support. They become victims of a system that offers no rehabilitation. Many re-offend - they have been shown no other path...

Zero Point (Aquarian Awakening)
The Transcendental Evolution Of Man
A transition from one form of energy to the next
A change of frequency and vibration
We share the pulse of all of existence
The sacred circuit
Everything being one
7.8 cycles per second
Increasing rapidly until they reach thirteen cycles per second
Higher frequencies resolving in more complex patterns
A major shift in physical and spiritual vibration
Changing to forms of light - not of this world
Change within a twinkling of the eye
The created shall become the creators
The truth will manifest...
(Revealed to me in a dream: 21-12-12)

OUTSIDE THE LINES

Abuse Of Process
31/10/12 - Manassah's birthday - my version of events.

Outside my front door I could hear a commotion and the sound of fireworks. I went into the street and saw my son and his friends backing away from a boy pointing ignited rockets and randomly firing them at the passing traffic. As we watched a car screeched to a halt - two men jumped out and rushed towards the youth.

One shouted. "Drop the fireworks and put your hands behind your back!" They were not in uniform and at no time stated that they were officers of the law. The boy dropped the fireworks and raised his hands in submission. PC1 stood to the left of the youth and held him. It was clear to everyone that the arrest was justified. Whilst the boy's hands were raised PC2 withdrew his ASP expandable baton and for no apparent reason struck the boy to the right side of his body: the boy was not resisting arrest. PC2 then struck again this time to the left side of the body.

PC1 handcuffed the boy's hands behind his back thusly incapacitating him. PC2 grabbed the boy by his throat and head-butted him in the face. "You black cunt".

I approached the situation. "What the fuck are you doing - stop - he is not resisting."
"I will do what I fucking want - he fired fireworks at us. Back off or you will be arrested."
"I saw what he did - but I am asking what the fuck are you doing?"

PC1 marched the boy off. PC2, instead of accompanying his colleague, stayed behind to argue with me and four or five kids (my son and his friends) who were now shouting abuse at him. He had no reason to stay behind yet started arguing back like a teenager, and not a very bright one. He was screaming at everyone to back off - out of control - extremely emotional. No one had approached him within two meters. Realising that he was no longer in a position of power PC2 became aggressive - he had lost control of the situation.

He approached me - ASP raised - shouting - "Back off" - placing his extended hand on my chest. "No."

I told my son and his friends to step back. PC2 stepped forward as if to strike me. I calmly made a suggestion - "Come on then" - he chose not to.

At this point PC1 returned. "Go - all of you just go." He was not aggressive and we all complied. My son and I entered our front garden and stood at the top of steps outside the front door.

Three police cars and a van pulled up - eleven officers were now on the scene. It came to light that the boy, still in handcuffs, had escaped. I could see PC2 getting agitated at the loss of his expensive cuffs - which he alone was financially responsible for. He walked away then stopped - turned to look at me - ran into my garden - up the steps - "I am nicking you."

My son blocked his path so that I could step into the house and shut the door. Had I of done so my son would have been arrested hence I stepped forward allowing the officer to grab my garments in the throat area. I did not resist yet in a physically aggressive state of rage PC2 pushed me down the stairs.

At street level I was told to lie on the floor - which I voluntarily did. Once on the floor PC1 and 2 were on me trying to hold me down with their knees: I was not resisting. They both then drew their ASPs - upon seeing this I grabbed their apparatus preventing them from striking me. They kept trying to raise the weapons but could not release them from my grasp.

PC1 - "Let go."
"Yeah - when you get off me."

He did as I asked and requested that I tell the approaching kids to back off - which I did. PC2 continued trying to strike me with no avail. I allowed my hands to be handcuffed behind my back. For no reason PC2 then once again placed his knees on me - one knee was on my throat. He proceeded to strike my shins, which stung like hell. The whole time I was shouting at the kids telling them not to get involved. They were angry at what they had seen and wanted to retaliate.

PC2 shouted at his fellow officers to arrest my son - who had actually done nothing wrong. I shouted at Manassah to run - fortunately he was too fast for them and got away. Two other officers marched me against a wall. PC2 approached and punched me twice in the chin: neither of the two officers happened to notice. I was taken to the station and charged with 'threatening behaviour with the intent to use unlawful violence and assault'.

My defence was simple. "I am a middle class - middle-aged - articulate - professional - why for no reason would I interfere with the law on behalf of a complete stranger? In my opinion I witnessed an abuse of power resulting in a violent racist attack - hence I was compelled to voice my objection."

The prosecution's main police witness was also the disclosure officer, thus in a position to pervert the course of justice - which he had done by withholding crucial evidence for my defence. The case had to be adjourned thrice until a new disclosing officer was appointed. Through the new appointee it became apparent that the two police officers had withheld crucial evidence, favourable towards myself, that had been supplied by an independent witness. This new evidence brought light to the fact that the police may have been abusing their power.

On the night in question there had been a police despatch recording regarding my case - "Two officers are beating the crap out of a man that was trying to stop them beating up a young black boy."

Fourth appearance. Before my case proceeded the clerk suggested to the police prosecutor that she might not wish to contest the 'Abuse Of Process' application. Due to blatant CPS and police negligence and numerous warnings from the court it was now highly unlikely that the prosecution would win the case. The prosecution lawyer said that she had already suggested to the CPS that they drop my case - "The CPS insists that I carry on regardless."

Although all seemed to be in my favour I was not putting any faith in the British justice system to prevail (UK law and justice do not seem to walk hand in hand). However, my defence team was marvellous - the court clerk astute to the law - the judge fair - the Crown Prosecutor of no apparent substance.

The judge's final comments, which he gave in writing, were damning to the police yet beneficial in my private prosecution case for assault and abuse of power.

In the meantime: word on the street was that PC2 had arrested a completely different boy for the same offence. I managed to contact the boy and put him in touch with my brief. I appeared in court as his witness - "That was not the boy firing fireworks at cars on the night in question." The case was thrown out of court.

OUTSIDE THE LINES

PC2 often physically abused young men - known on the street as 'Charlie Essex'. He was a bullying scumbag of a man. Had I known at the time that this was the pig that had previously had his hands around my son's throat things may have turned out slightly different.

The upside of this saga - I received £12,000 police compensation and PC 'Charlie Essex' (a decorated officer) resigned from the police force. Apparently his next venture was as a male stripper…

Westfield 76
July 2014 - State murder of Eric Garner - 'I Can't Breathe'.
August 2014 - State murder of Michael Brown - 'Hands Up Don't Shoot'.

November 2014 - As the winter nights drew in I started to question why I was still attending and documenting the protests outside the American Embassy in Grosvenor Square. It was cold, dark and the building was empty. Basically a bunch of people standing in a backstreet of London chanting to each other whilst the rest of the world went about its business oblivious of our protest.

Until my ban (the threat of extreme harassment) I attended most London protests merely to document. My belief being that marching, protesting and petitioning on the whole achieves nothing. Protesting outside the American Embassy was clearly fruitless.

I openly voiced my opinion - 'nothing was being achieved here'. I suggested somewhere more public - a commercial high street - a shopping centre - a place to be seen and demonstrate Civil Unrest.

I received notification from the 'London Black Revs' that on December 10th

Memoirs Of A Naughty Boy #2

Shot In The Westfield Shopping Centre

there was to be a protest at Westfield shopping centre in Shepherd's Bush. The plan was for all to gather at 7pm and to the sound of a horn burst all were to descend to the floor chanting 'Hands up don't shoot' followed by 'I can't breathe'. In theory this sounded like a plan - although I was doubtful that suddenly there would be a mass descent to the ground.

Before attending my girlfriend offered me a lift.
"Nah - I'm gonna get the tube."
"The tube? You never take the underground."
"I was gonna drive but if I am arrested I will get a parking ticket in the morning."
"Oh!"
At this time she did not know me too well.

OUTSIDE THE LINES

I hovered around Westfield - recognising very few: just a couple of Facebook friends. The area was full of middle-class shoppers and tourists. I was now even more dubious at the possibility of a successful protest.

7pm on the dot - 'BAUGH' - a loud claxon horn was set off and indeed hundreds of people hit the floor.

"We can't breathe"
"We can't breathe"
"We can't breathe"
"Hands up don't shoot"
"Hands up don't shoot"
"Hands up don't shoot"
"No justice no peace"
"No justice no peace"
"No justice no peace"

An immediate success. In rushed the police but they were stuck, the protesters were not the 'black unruly students' that they were expecting. No - these were predominately white middle-class - this was a fashionable protest that was trending on social media. There would be no police brutality - no batons drawn - no one thrown to the floor by a gang of police - no one handcuffed - no one dragged away. The police had to back off and reassess the situation.

As I wandered around taking photos, filming and watching the police peacefully try to disperse small pockets of protesters that were lying on the floor, only to be faced by another group only a few metres away and then another and another. This protest was working - it was gaining momentum and the police were seemingly helpless.

We had the run of Westfield - the police had backed off. Of course as in all protests there were those with alternative motives: anarchists - a necessary evil. No major press coverage on peaceful protest - things needed to be broken for front-page news. According to the newspapers 'windows were smashed and security guards assaulted'. The press as always made things up as they went along - dramatizing the whole event, quelling any mass sympathy and playing into the hands of the police.

After parading around Westfield for a few hours we proceeded to march around Shepherd's Bush Green where there were many speakers explaining the reason for such protest. A group of us strolled back towards the shopping centre, which was by now cordoned off by hundreds of police. We were coerced toward the roundabout where the police proceeded to surround and kettle us into a three policemen deep circle. There was no escaping unless one was deemed in need of medical attention. If you needed to pee it was 'unlucky'. During this time I was sharing info with my girlfriend who was relaying it to my Facebook followers. Before my FB account was removed, for having 'too much traffic', I had 5,000 friends and 8,000 followers. She in return was telling me that the kettled group was being reported on the news.

Three hours later we were individually filmed for facial recognition (which I can assure is most effective) and taken one at a time by a designated police person to sit on a bus. I sat at the front of the upper deck and waited as each arrestee went through this process. After an hour or so we were driven to a special police-holding unit in Wandsworth to be processed. The bus was absolutely freezing. Seeing as there were quite a few buses I realised this was going to take a while: by this time my need to pee was urgent. I cunningly explained to the officer that I was an older gentleman with kidney problems (I lied) and being unable to pee could cause medical complications - he was compliant.

OUTSIDE THE LINES

Once in the warmth of the police station, and having relieved myself, I (again cunningly) suggested to the policeman that it might be a good idea if instead of us both going back onto the freezing cold bus for a few more hours, perhaps we should just nip through the door to the charging area. He could process me and go home and I could be taken to a warm cell. Again he was wisely compliant.

I was held for 12 hours and charged with 'Public Order Offences' - which if found guilty could hold up to an eight-year prison sentence. I had actually committed no crime and the CCTV would depict me walking around with my camera. However, that threat hung over me for next fourteen months.

In all seventy six of us were arrested for the same offence. A 'Westfield 76' committee was set up for regular meetings. We discussed the case and volunteer solicitors assured us that the matter would be dropped - 'No Further Action'.

Personally I did not give a crap and found the middle-class liberal minded group comforting not to my taste. We were protesting regarding the murders of innocent men at the hands of the police yet these people were seeking counselling after one night in the cells.

The long and the short of it: I was given an 'NFA' notice - however, due to facial recognition I have been threatened and harassed by the police at many following protests.

When an atrocity happens in America we in the UK march and protest because it is trending on social media: 'Hands Up Don't Shoot' - 'I Can't Breathe' - but most remain silent when the atrocity is home grown...

Memoirs Of A Naughty Boy #2

OUTSIDE THE LINES

Upon Reflection
Instantly accessible freely available information
Coming to terms with fading supremacy
The noblest acts
The most horrific atrocities
The problem is systemic
Insufficient human rights
Lack of respect
Make the pie bigger so that everyone has a bigger piece
How has the dream become so distorted?
Profit transcends race
Wipe out debt
Start from a clean slate
Socialism for the rich
Capitalism for the poor
Serve yourself and simultaneously serve others
I am not a person of despair I am a person of hope
Someone has to take the blame
The fundamental belief is that wealth is to be shared
Those who contribute the least take the most
They tell you what they want and you accept
Humans can change what humans create
From an empty world to a full world
Tax on consumption not income
State terrorism
The end of the benefit from economic growth
Rethink the definition of progress
More growth creates more poverty
Operating within a rigged tax system
A perverse course of human destiny

Crypto-currency the new incentive
Capitalism is not to blame
We have a deceptive form of capitalism
Evermore diminishing yields are unevenly distributed
Human beings can be bought or sold
Dependant on constant growth to service debt
Only some of us know
Human beings come to their senses slowly and individually
An unsustainable asset growth
The system of money is an abused man-made law
We now have to start all over again…

Obama
I perceive Obama to have been the best president that America has ever produced - however, has no less blood on his hands than any other.

Within his presidency the Obama administration was complicit in America bombing Iraq - Afghanistan - Pakistan - Somalia - Yemen - Libya - Syria. Although his intention before being elected was to rid the world of nuclear weapons, Obama continued to commission the construction of nuclear arms.

2009 - President Obama was awarded the Nobel Peace Prize for his promise to help 'rid the world of nuclear weapons'…

Hilary Clinton
Had Hilary Clinton won the presidency she had guaranteed a war with Iran and intended to continue Nixon's 'War On Drugs' - a bill also championed by her husband's administration which had incarcerated more young black men

than any other regime since the Transatlantic Slave Trade. She was also the architect of the 1994 'Three Strikes' and life imprisonment bill...

Black Pride
The 1960s Civil Rights movement saw positive change: 'Black Power' - 'Black Is Beautiful' - 'Black Consciousness'. All this was damaged in the early 1970s by Nixon's 'War On Drugs' (war on black people) - which occurred simultaneously with the influx of opiates and cocaine base into black communities.

Trump
July 2015 - I placed a bet on Donald Trump to win the U.S. presidency. I was ridiculed, belittled and laughed at. Even as the polls peaked and troughed I was confident of a Trump victory. My intelligent girlfriend, who was originally in total agreement, was starting to doubt our perception. It was not looking good yet I still felt he would win. However, when he did indeed win I could not believe it. Although my winnings were £1300 it was a sour victory.

Trump Is The Result
We are now experiencing the results of a country born out of genocide and upon the backs of slaves - with a continued history of racial intolerance and outmoded gun laws.

America's contamination by The Transatlantic Slave Trade and is homogeneous to nuclear waste - it will take thousands of years to decay - until that time all that come in contact shall become cancerous - thus the continued feeding of recycled hatred.

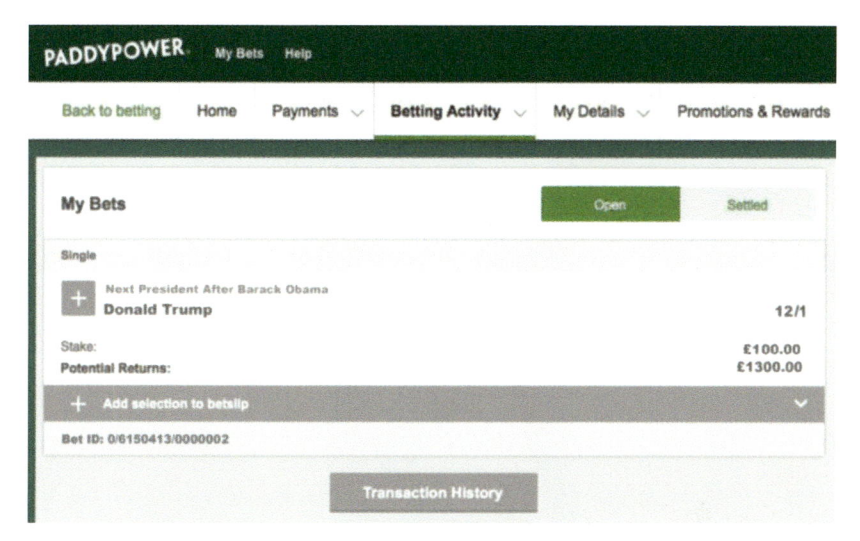

Bet Placed 18 Months Earlier

I perceive that none of this is the result of Trump - Trump is the result of America...

Wumni Girl

2015 - A conversation between Ibiwunmi Olaiya - the original Soul II Soul dancer and dance floor icon - and myself. Two dancers - I have never referred to myself as a dancer before but in this case it seems appropriate - who in 30 years have only ever communicated via movement and vision: never a word uttered.

Wumni: - *"You really are an inspiration. As I looked at the cover of your book and it hit me, there is a man there who keeps daring himself to boldly go where he has never been and live his dream as he dreams it! See I know that person - every step I take is a dare to myself to go ahead and live it! Funny we never really chatted back in the day. Truth be told I too spoke to very few people on the dance/club scene, but I*

OUTSIDE THE LINES

Wumni - Soul II Soul

knew of you. You were very difficult to miss. You wore the expression as I wore - 'don't mess with me'. Yet you were fascinating in how you carried yourself and yes how you danced. You then went on to have your own clothing line and band! Now a book that shares an insight into what it was like. A wicked book - riveting poignant - touching - funny. Yes, I thoroughly enjoyed your insights into that era. I can see a movie based on this book."

Me: "I first saw you at the Wag on a Wednesday night - circa 1986. You were wearing a khaki army jacket fastened with a black belt and a khaki officer's cap and very little else - I thought you were hot."

Wumni: *"Barrie, those little nothings that I used to wear were vintage 1950s*

2018 - Celebrating The Life Of Paul Trouble Anderson

swimming costumes - I collected them like crazy. They were mini dresses with built in knickers - I lived for them! Perfect for club dancing - the dance floor was my stage and church. Good times...!"

The Coconut Cutters
One Man - One Machete - One Coconut

Nu-age British Grafters not afraid to get their hands dirty - getting the odd cut and bruise: up with the lark. Dickensian style Costermongers hawking their wares.

Chop ~ Chop ~ Chop: three chops of the machete and off with the top of the coconut - a straw inserted and the fresh water drunk.

Benny Thorpe built a reliable team of street savvy young men to man his

OUTSIDE THE LINES

2016 - TCC - Attired In Sharpeye

operation of supplying fresh coconuts on his self-created pitches in the London Street markets: in the tradition of working class street vendors.

Instead of the stereotypicle 'young men of colour' (that the media like to paint) these ambitious young men got up off their butts and made their own way in the world - with their own positive work ethos.

Costa Rican organic coconuts - the bi-product turned into charcoal - no waste and totally biodegradable. All these young dudes need to achieve their goal is a fresh box of coconuts and a machete - no artificial power needed - only the warmth and light of the sun.

Manassah's Story In Short
Due to the internal politics of youth my son decided to go it alone. He secured himself a prime pitch upon the Portobello Road and on market day he pitched up.

Of course it was I that had to get up at 3am to go to New Spitalfields Fruit and Veg market to purchase the fresh jellied coconuts - and I that had to take him to Portobello at 6am to set up stall.

Due to circumstances beyond control Manassah had changed his machete at the last minute to the large kitchen knife that I usually used for coconut chopping: at his request I sharpened it. The result of using an unchartered blade was catastrophic. The knife deflected and slid off of the coconut that he was cutting and sliced into his wrist - the blood discharged like a fountain. The cool headedness of Manassah and quick thinking by Dougie, a market stallholder, had his arm wrapped in a T-shirt and held above his head. Whilst two people were separately calling 999 Dougie stopped a car on the Portobello

OUTSIDE THE LINES

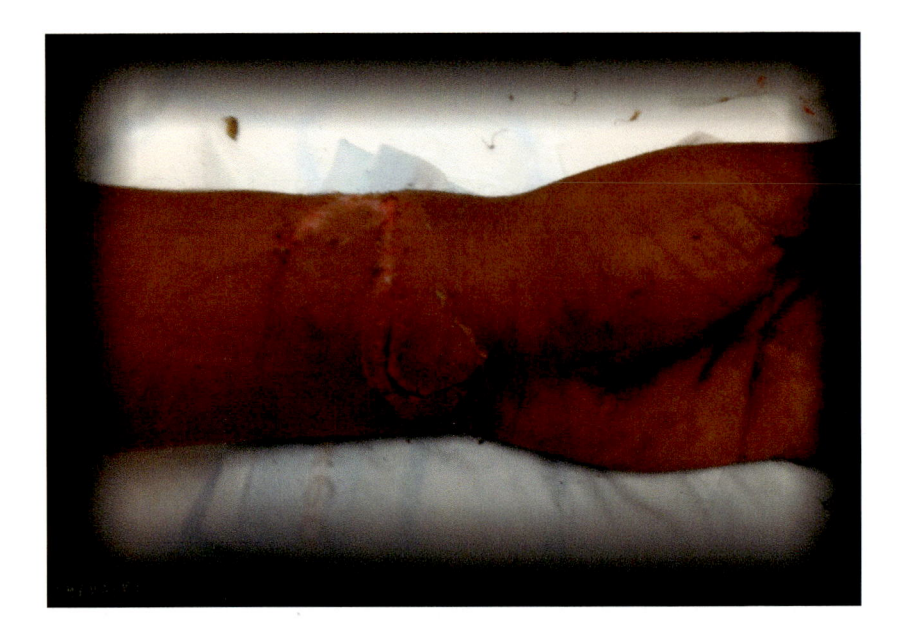

Road and asked the driver, whom he knew, to take Manassah to the hospital. Apparently he would have bled out if he had waited for the ambulance.

By some miracle the cut stopped short of his three main arteries - only one was slightly lacerated thus so much blood. The main worry at this point was the possibility of nerve damage - however, all fingers were functional. Manassah had to have a major operation: microsurgery performed by a notable plastic surgeon. He was very cool and calm throughout the whole ordeal - possibly due to shock: this may have saved his life. He only had one question. "Am I going to die…?"

Shot At Spitalfields By Chris Tang

An Honest Days Graft
Minimalist Utilitarian Dandyism: I turn up - I sell - I go home.

Six years earlier I had closed all five of my London Sharpeye stores intent on retirement. As far as I was concerned the game was over - it was time to get out - I was tired of working merely to pay the landlords.

Of course I did not retire at all, but continued to design capsule collections: '1-in-Ten' - (ten per style - per colour) and highly successful it was/is.

OUTSIDE THE LINES

My experience of helping my son with his fresh coconut water stall on Portobello Road Market - going to New Spitalfields fruit market at 3am for fresh coconuts, then helping him set up stall at 6am - opened my eyes to the realisation that I thoroughly enjoyed it. It felt like the way forward - a completion of the full circle - a return to what I knew: the street market.

I started a pitch (Saturdays & Sundays) in Spitalfields Old Market (St. Mary's Hospital Fields) - where I played as a kid. I was already selling my limited edition collections online to capacity - I missed the personal interaction with people, hence back to the street it was. I continued to fall uphill...

Freedom Of Choice
Universal suffrage: the right for everyone to be involved to the same level in the political agenda of one's nation. It does not mean that one is obligated to take part in a five yearly secret ballot.

Women fought and died for our 'Freedom Of Choice'.

Voting for corruption makes one a part of the problem - hence one has no right to complain. If one does not vote because one does not feel represented one has every right to complain: indeed it is one's duty to do so. No one should be voting for something in which they do not believe - that would be self-harm.

Freedom of choice means freedom of choice - it is my civil right to choose not to vote if that is what I wish. No one has the right to tell me any different. By telling me 'you have to vote' you take away my freedom of choice!

Show me an honest non-corrupt politician that represents me and he or she shall have my vote. Which politician stands for the common man?

Memoirs Of A Naughty Boy #2

2017 - JC - London

I do not claim to understand politics nor fathom its workings.

To many people's abhorrence before the rise of Jeremy Corbyn I had never voted - previously I felt unrepresented. I don't want the lesser of two evils - I want no evil at all.

My knowledgeable girlfriend (at the time) made me aware of JC. I had been waiting for a political leader with certain qualities - hoping that we had a representative of the people with the character I look for in a person: fairness - liberty - equality - honesty - justice - compassion.

OUTSIDE THE LINES

One may have the right to vote - however, it is one's duty to think!

Tory supporters back their party regardless of personalities - whereas Labour supporters are petty and will sell out the party over personalities and personal issues rather then support the party's political policies - hence Labour lost themselves the last election.

The ruling class rule by dividing the working class - the ironic outcome is the 'Working Class Tory'…

The Way I See It
It is tough to inspire students who are part of a fast growing throw away culture. However, this was/is my intention: not to teach - rather to exchange knowledge. These students can teach me as much I can teach them. This first came to light about ten years ago when lecturing at the RCA (Royal College of Art) - these students were already designers (the very reason why they were there in the first place). There was no aspect of design that I could share with them or even wished to: my design method/process is unique to me as theirs is to them.

Every designer - artist - creative is an individual with the need and desire to create his or her own path and then walk along it without judgement.

What I do bestow upon them is my thirty-five years of experience in the industry. I advise of the pitfalls - positives - negatives - successes - failures: I have experienced them all and am able to articulate it in a fashion that other creative minds can relate to…

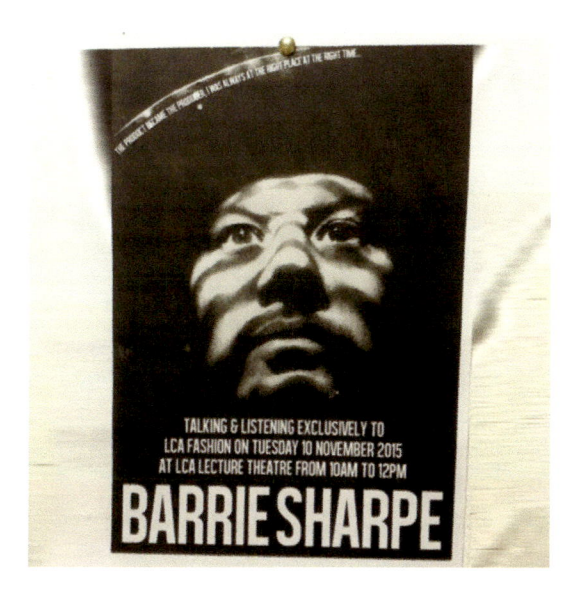

Lecturing Skills And Method (Leeds College Of Art)
Not being a confident public speaker and with almost zero preparation I was slightly unnerved when setting my eyes upon the huge room filled with one hundred and thirty students and six lecturers - all waiting to hear me speak. When seeing the size of my audience I exclaimed "Oh Shit" to Sam (previously a trainee at Duffer) the programme leader who was about to introduce me. Fortunately, as I hoped, I was received with a barrage of questions kicked off by the lecturers - once I started addressing each question the information exchange flowed for 2hrs. I felt that I was brutally honest about the industry and also regarding my part in the game - without actually disillusioning my questioners: hopefully inspiring a few…

OUTSIDE THE LINES

Royal College of Art

20th October 2008

Lecture At The Royal of Art Fashion Menswear Department

Dear Barrie

We are pleased that you accepted the position and look forward to hearing you lecture.

Commencing November 10th

The timetable will start at 10am and with a one-hour break for lunch you should be finished by 4pm. There are eleven 2nd year fashion students that I'd like you to see and one of those is a footwear designer. You are required you to listen to what each student has to say about the work they are doing and to give them feedback on their design and toile work in progress.

I'd really like you to encourage them to think through the logistics of what they are doing, in terms of achievability, commerciality and practicality. Obviously from your point of view and not necessarily from a biased fashion only perspective. You'll see things you relate to and others you don't so it stands to reason that certain objectivity is required.

You will need to bring in your passport – this is needed for all new lecturers to get you on the payroll.

Best wishes

Ike Rust

Memoirs Of A Naughty Boy #2

In Conversation With Barrie K Sharpe

Diana Donaldson (Course Leader and Associate Lecturer at Central St. Martins and London College of Fashion) Jan 2018 - *I invited Barrie Sharpe to speak to students from Central St. Martins and the London College of Fashion because he is an inclusive, successful creative who does not play by the rules. The creative industry has never been more competitive. I wanted my students to learn about the power of an alternative and diverse approach.*

Once you can get him to talk, Barrie Sharpe has a lot to say. He insists he was just lucky; 'I fell uphill'. As someone who believes there's no such thing as luck, I see it differently. I believe in opportunity, the ability to see it in the first instance and the

OUTSIDE THE LINES

awareness to act in such moments.

Sharpe has an innate ability to see and seize opportunity, more importantly, the readiness to act at any given time. He is always prepared. He never stops. It seems to be a continuum of ever evolving creativity; one quality project after the next. Without fear of failure, without seeking celebrity, high profit margins nor approval. 'It is what it is because I want it that way' was the uncompromising message none of the students expected to hear but all have responded to positively.

They gasped and applauded at the last frame, of the screening of 90s iconic record The Masterplan, as Barrie K Sharpe and Diana Brown hit the dance floor simultaneously in the splits. Students later queued to speak to Barrie, touch the Sharpeye products and look through his book - 'This Was Not Part Of The Masterplan'.

Once they had a grasp of the measure of the man, his accomplishments and that he demonstrates the belief in his convictions, they see him as relevant today as he always was, and understand his enduring legacy.

The most encouraging feedback from students was focused around Sharpe's journey. They realised that if they take a genuine look further than what is current, there lies a wealth of knowledge, authentic expertise and inspiration that can be regenerated and made into their own: a similar process for a different time...

Memoirs Of A Naughty Boy #2

2019 - With Rochelle - Shot By Kenny Wellington

Kavos - Rochelle

2019 - Walking along the beach under the hot Kavos sun minding my own business - an attractive lady approaches me.

"Hello Barrie."

"Hello." I cautiously reply.

"You don't know who I am do you?"

"No"

OUTSIDE THE LINES

"It's me - Rochelle - the girl that you claim to have been in love with when we were at school: I read your book."

She then gives me the warm kiss on the lips that I had been waiting forty-eight years for. We sat by the sea and spoke through the afternoon and into the night until sunrise...

BJ
January 2018 - I placed a bet on Boris Johnson to become the next British prime minister.

Again: I was ridiculed - belittled - laughed at.
Again: as the polls peaked and troughed I was confident of a BJ victory.
Again: it was not looking good yet I still felt he would win.
Again: although my winnings were £900 it was a sour victory.

Within the period of me placing the bet and his victory BJ lost favour with the UK populace and it seemed apparent that he would not become our next PM. Through much deception and jiggery pokery he managed pull it off. July 2019 Boris Johnson became the prime minister of Great Britain....

Brexit Turmoil
For the first 24hrs I was actually all for Brexit - fortunately my smart girlfriend soon put me straight to the facts and the communal rise of outspoken racism sealed it for me. Stupidly I did not vote either way.

In my defence: until my smart girlfriend revealed Jeremy Corbyn to me I had never voted for anything.

PADDYPOWER

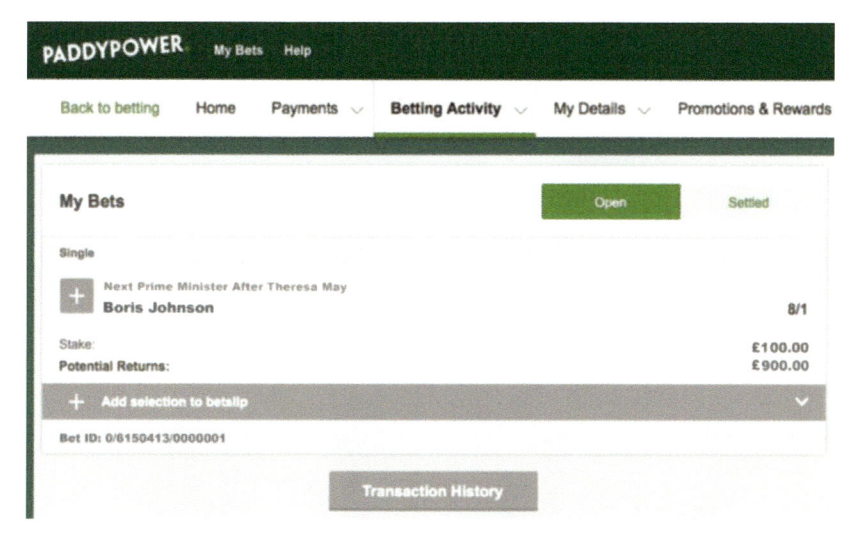

My Bets

Single		
Next Prime Minister After Theresa May		
Boris Johnson		8/1
Stake:		£100.00
Potential Returns:		£900.00

Bet ID: 0/6150413/0000001

Bet Placed 17 Months Earlier

My issue with Europe was the steady rise of the far right - but it seemed that the far right was already here. Had I voted 'out' I would now have to account myself responsible for empowering this overwhelming swarm of racism that is currently sweeping across the UK.

We are all accountable for our actions - unfortunately it will be our children who are going to reap the misfortunes that we have bestowed upon them. I do not blame all those that voted leave - we were all lied to: I was fortunate enough to have the advice of someone that knew everything...

OUTSIDE THE LINES

State Manipulation Of The Masses

I do not particularly support Muslims - Blacks - Women - Gays - Lesbians - Arabs - Native Americans - Jews - Irish (nor any other persecuted group). I do not have to particularly like anyone to oppose his or her oppression. I am for equality: I dislike most people equally. My fight is against global - national - regional - local injustice. I merely use logic: if you are willing to participate in persecuting any group of people - next you may wish to persecute me.

Throughout history there has always been an imposed 'enemy' - a 'threat to society' - Communists - Blacks - Asians - Jews - Homosexuals - Women - Irish - Disabled: now 'Islamic Fundamentalists'…

Memoirs Of A Naughty Boy #2

They divide us
Distort our beliefs
Furnish us with lies
Imprison our minds
Refuse us our rights
Enslave us with debt
Deny us our freedom
Control our thoughts
Demonise the minority
Entice us with promises
Indoctrinate our children
Turn our empathy to hate
Reward us with possessions
Propaganda will become truth
We will be rendered blind - deaf - dumb...

The Division
Religion
Politics
Gender
Wealth
Colour
Class
Race...

OUTSIDE THE LINES

Stuck
Anxiety = stuck in the future
Depression = stuck in the past
Anxiety + Depression = stuck in the present.

My life may seem contradictory. Sometimes I get stuck - I struggle with life - work - my son - people - relationships - society. It is like running on ice: no matter how fast I run I cannot get away. I try to get over it (I know I should) - I have a strong mind, which to an extent I can control. I attempt to move forward but the density of life is often impregnable - thusly denying my progress. I lose a grip of my reality and my logic - stuck in deep thought. The weight of life becomes immensely heavy - a load sometimes too hard to bear; yet I have to bear - I have responsibilities - I have a son to watch over (it is my job).

The simplest of tasks become a colossal burden: making a phone call - paying a bill - going to the bank - emptying the bin. Mentally and physically debilitating - draining me of life. I do not wish to face the day - I wake at 5am: thinking - yet avoiding reality. Trapped inside my mind - logical thought in a distant haze. I cannot leave - my son needs me.

I seek solace in creativity - I throw myself into projects intensely: stopping only to eat or carry out quick menial tasks. Eventually I have to return to face the responsibilities of life and parenthood. I incessantly seek creativity to escape the pains of everyday life.

Look at my face it may seem that I am smiling
Look into my eyes you will see I am crying
Feel my heart - deep inside my soul is dying...

Finally

For as long I can remember I did not fit in. I lived from day-to-day: sometimes happy and sometimes sad. No plans, merely living in the moment. I took risks - I weighed up my options - good or bad I would always proceed fearlessly. I put little value upon myself or my safety - willing to gamble all on a whim: I usually won.

Until my son Manassah was born I felt very alone - his birth gave me purpose: I was 33 years old.

I fell into the fatherhood mantle quite comfortably and although I had no role models on the correct ways to bring up a man-child, I certainly knew what not to do. I knew I had to keep him close, safe and for him to be my main focus in life.

Manassah's mother left me 18 months later. Although sad and lonely I did not falter with my son's well being: I remained consistent. For me to focus on my son I left Duffer - walked out on my record deal - left my band - abandoned my sponsorship from Levi's.

OUTSIDE THE LINES

I really had to grow up. I bought a reasonably priced four-story house in Camden and set up a lifestyle where my son would always come first. It was not easy and often a solitary task. Many nights I cried in despair - I feared (my first real experience of fear) that I was not giving Manassah all the emotional love that he needed. My love was masculine and I knew it was lacking in many ways. He got all the kisses and cuddles he desired yet I could not give the motherly love that only a woman can provide.

To be clear: his mother was still in the picture - due to her work commitments, location and time inflexibility it was convenient for me to be the main carer.

Owing to the previously mentioned slippery move by the Japanese I brought Sharpeye home to Soho and created a successful wholesale operation. Whilst doing all of this Manassah still came first. I started work after taking him to nursery and finished in time to collect him.

I spent much time providing for his needs: perhaps too much time. I feel I may have given too much, spoiled him and possibly overcompensated for what I perceived were my shortfalls.

As stated - a solitary time for me - I could not hold down a meaningful relationship and floundered from one woman to another with no offer of commitment. Eventually I realised it was futile trying to create such a bond when my focus was clearly elsewhere: hence I stopped trying.

As Manassah got older and I became surplus to requirements - I focused more on my work - opened more stores - started writing and recording songs again - built bicycles and motorbikes.

Again I felt alone - distant from people - merely living from day to day. I

Sharpeye 1952 Harley Davidson Hydra Glide

realised how much damage my dysfunctional childhood had caused.

A recent email message from my sister - who now lives in Canada. *'Something's been on my mind for a long time now, it's about how I treated you when we were kids; I just want to say that I am so very sorry'…*

2014 - I Met An Intriguing Intelligent Woman
Possibly the most intelligent and to me the most important person I have ever met: she knew everything about everything. She convinced me that we fitted - indeed we did fit (for the first time in my life I felt that I truly fitted in). Plans were made for our future: we were going to grow old together. I had never felt like this before. I wanted to spend time with her, laugh with her, converse with

OUTSIDE THE LINES

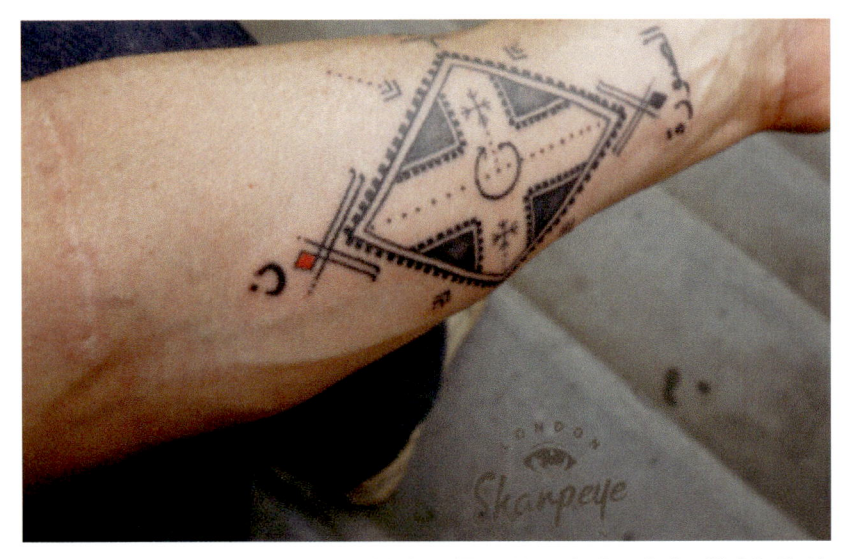

Arabic Compass - To Assure That I Never Get Lost Again - Work By Tat2fx

her and most importantly be taught by her: she taught me much. I had reason to plan and now started living for tomorrow as well as just today. I looked forward to seeing her - she became my purpose. Her confidence in me gave me confidence in myself.

I loved this woman - I trusted her - I belonged - I was whole.

After a two and a half year whirlwind of laughter and joy - as quickly as it blossomed it faded - I lost the person who I thought I was going to spend the rest of my life with.

Doors in my head that had been freshly opened are now once again closed.

She was my happy place…

Worldwide Black Lives Matter Movement 2020

The following is merely my account of events - due to innumerable situations happening simultaneously many will have their own alternative accounts and experiences.

The BLM London kids fighting the old racist detritus had no idea that they were making history - changing the world and altering their futures.

Due to the Coronavirus and the lockdown - May 25th - on TV the world saw a black man publicly lynched in America by the very people sworn to protect him.

The focus was overwhelming - the whole world cried - stood up - marched - protested. The biggest Civil Rights outcry since the late 1960s.

May 31st - Black Lives Matter UK responded with an impromptu protest in London's Trafalgar Square. A strong turnout with a wide representation of varied races - colours - religions: the rest of the world followed suit. I attended to support and visually document.

June 3rd - The next BLM protest was in London's Hyde Park - circa eighty thousand attended, a glorious event with varied races - colours - religions: the rest of the world followed suit. I attended to support and visually document.

June 6th - Parliament Square - more people than the eye could see - again the varied races - colours - religions: the rest of the world followed suit. I attended to support and visually document.

June 7th - American Embassy; the area came to a standstill due to the monumental capacity of the crowd. We marched to Parliament Square and then onto Trafalgar Square. Once more, varied races - colours - religions: the rest of

OUTSIDE THE LINES

BLM Protest - 7th June 2020 - Whitehall

the world followed suit. I attended to support and visually document.

The following week Tommy Robinson was up in arms claiming that in Bristol BLM had torn down the statue of the slave trader and Tory MP Edward Colston and thrown it into the harbour waters. He further claimed that BLM had graffitied 'Racist' upon the statue of Sir Winston Churchill in Parliament Square. Neither of these statues were desecrated by BLM. The Colston felling was shown live on TV and clearly not BLM. Churchill was graffitied in front of my very eyes and not by BLM. TR aired a video on social media calling all English Defence League supporters and the Football Lads Alliance to band together and come to London to protect the statues from a thus far non-planned BLM protest in Parliament Square on the 13th June. This clearly incited the less intelligent to take up his call to arms and blindly join his 'righteous' cause: it suited their narrative.

Memoirs Of A Naughty Boy #2

BLM Protest - 31st May 2020 - Trafalgar Square

Upon hearing Tommy Robinson's demand for patriots to rally together in protection of our national monuments BLM UK cancelled a protest planned for the same day in Hyde Park.

11th June - The London Black Revolutionaries announced that they would be holding a protest in Parliament Square on the 13th: meeting at Hyde Park and marching down via Trafalgar Square.

On the Saturday I cycled down early to join the protesters at Trafalgar. As only a few had arrived I rode down Whitehall to see how many of TR's army had turned up. I was taken aback - there were literally thousands of drunken old men shouting racist abuse and guzzling copious amounts of beer.

Whitehall had been cut in half by two separate crowd barriers manned by a

OUTSIDE THE LINES

BLM Protest - 6th June - Parliament Square

hundred or so riot gear clad police officers - this ensured that neither side could clash.

I returned to the Square - I guess at most there were about two hundred of us. The regular chants were chanted:
'Black lives matter'
'I can't breathe'
'Hands up don't shoot'
'Police are the murderers'
Etcetera.

First I heard the shouting - then the monkey noises - then the volley of noise grenades - then saw fireworks and smoke bombs being hurled at us - next the

BLM Protest - 13th June - Trafalgar Square

shattering of broken bottles all around our feet. We were totally surrounded with no way out. Literally thousands of right wing tooled up football thugs.

Although potentially terrifying no one seemed perturbed by the desperate circumstances that we had found ourselves in.

The situation was tense - nonetheless the small circle of BLM defenders stood their ground and waited for the onslaught. Tommy's patriot army kept charging in small numbers only to be repelled by the defenders who where also protecting women and children shielded in the circle.

Caught in the moment many of the younger men broke rank to get their hands on one or two of the agitators and beat the crap out of them. People shouted for

OUTSIDE THE LINES

BLM Protest - 13th June - Trafalgar Square - Returning A Smoke Bomb

the youngsters to come back - on their own they were targets and it weakened the central circle.

Before long it was a full on running battle - despite the fact that BLM were heavily outnumbered on each encounter the attackers still ran away. I attended to support and visually document - however, I was given no choice - I had to defend myself: whilst doing so I captured the situation on my iPhone live to Facebook.

This went on for two hours - the thugs charged, BLM repelled - cut off with numbers falling (somehow some had escaped the Square) with no visible way out. Out of nowhere the marchers arrived from Hyde Park - they had been kettled for an hour unable to reach the square - at least three hundred of them. The

BLM Protest - 13th June - Trafalgar Square

tables turned and although still heavily outnumbered the hooligans were chased all around the immediate vicinity.

It also came to light that a vast number of BLM marchers from South London had been prevented from crossing bridges and had gathered at Waterloo. The EDL/FLA made their way to Waterloo Station - they went to hurt and intimidate yet it was they that got served.

Warnings had been announced for BLM supporters not to attend in case of such trouble and the risk of the press tainting the peaceful protests. Fortunately in BLM's favour the savage racists brutally attacked the police at every given chance - national and international TV crews filmed these confrontations for the world to see. The PM, racist newspapers and the police had no

OUTSIDE THE LINES

BLM Protest - 13th June - Trafalgar Square

choice other than to publicly condemn the EDL/FLA as 'Racist Thugs'. As far as I am concerned that was a victory. Protest is imperative - the world saw the UK for what it really is - an embarrassment.

Gianna Floyd (aged 6) *"Daddy Changed The World."* George Floyd payed the ultimate price that may change the lives of many.

Due to the worldwide protests George Floyd's murderer had his charge upgraded from 3rd to 2nd-degree murder and was subsequently found to be guilty. The three other cops present, whom previously had not had any charges imposed upon them, were also charged with 2nd-degree murder. The New York city council was compelled to approve a bill to ban the local police force from using the 'chokehold' manoeuvre: many other US cities followed suit.

Had the worldwide BLM protests not taken place Derek Chauvin would still be a serving police officer instead of serving twenty two and half years in prison.

(To be clear)
I Turn Up Take Photos/Document and Go Home
I am not an activist
I know nothing of politics
I am affiliated with no groups
I will support any protest against injustice - no matter to whom or by whom…

OUTSIDE THE LINES

BLM Protest - 6th June 2021 - Parliament Square - Shot By Steve Proctor

Memoirs Of A Naughty Boy #2

Life has disappointed me - perhaps I disappointed life - however, I have certainly lived it on my terms and have left my mark upon the universe...

To sum it all up: I changed the game by not playing - Barrie Sharpe

The End

OUTSIDE THE LINES

I
Although not looking
I found you
I was not wanting
Yet you gave
You shared your damaged soul
I forgot my pain
It was not only you with a need to heal
I let go
I saw through you
It was I that would fix you
Wanting nothing in return
I would evolve
I would take control
Commitment without committing
I did it for me
I no longer want your rejection
Together we were still…

II
My mind is my prison
You are there in my head
In my mind
I cope
Distract my thoughts
Yet again you return to torture me with your indifference
I was once your king
You talked to me
You understood me (perhaps you did not)
Taught me

Memoirs Of A Naughty Boy #2

We laughed
Now I am nothing
You laugh and smile for others
Speak to others
Teach others
I no longer wish to speak
I no longer smile
Toil to laugh
Standing on the outside looking in
A Stranger
Ostracized
Alone and lonely
Confused
What occurred I know not of
You were there by my side
Loyal
Loving
Then gone
I live merely day-to-day
Struggling
Waiting to die
You were my saviour
Now the architect of my pain
You watched me fall
With each new character a new mask
Which were you…?

III
I stand in the face of the sun
Constant beaming light cast shadow in my wake

OUTSIDE THE LINES

My shadow is my past
Memories are my reasons to celebrate life
In the far distance the earth and sky meet
My destination
The wind will enrich my body with its unbounded power
Flowing tears of joy will cleanse my soul
I walk the path of freedom...

Protocol
No socks
No Jewellery
No 'men's perfumes'
Rolex or military watch
Cleanse oneself regularly
Only follow manly pursuits
One does not roll up one's sleeves
Never pull one's pants up too high
Trousers must have two back pockets
A smart hat holds a man in good stead
Skinny-leg jeans are not for grown men
Double-breasted blazers - six buttons - two side vents
Single-breasted jacket - three/four buttons - centre vent
As a rule no belt - Sharpeye pants have adjustable side straps
There is never a need to wear neither suit nor tie unless one wishes
When not wearing Sharpeye Levi 501s and classic shoes will suffice
Never sport an item of clothing that one is not comfortable wearing
All buttons done up at all times unless wishing to urinate or have sex
Boxers not Y-fronts - never wear boxers on the outside of one's trousers...

Memoirs Of A Naughty Boy #2

Code
Trust only one's father
Fear the man not the gun
Only tell what needs to be told
Never back yourself into a corner
The man with the scar is the victim
Do not play poker with a blind man
Never trust a man who always smiles
The man who is in prison got caught
Never fight a battle that cannot be won
If a man is not one's friend he may well be one's enemy
If one is going to risk imprisonment be sure it is worth it
The man who threatens you has already shown you his hand...

*31 January 2013 -
Created By Jon Daniel For
My Birthday*

Kids born in the 60s - grew up in the 70s - were the innovators of the 80s: then it all flat-lined_____!

OUTSIDE THE LINES

61 Years Old & Retired - Still: Creative - Prolific - Tenacious - Shot By Benny OSU

Memoirs Of A Naughty Boy #2

Ladies In Order Of Appearance

Kathy McIntosh spellchecker #1

Judy Bolton helped reason my words

Marie Harvey Harris corrected the corrections

Rose Boyt made sure all was ship shape and ready to sail

Jane Daniel (once again) layout

Editing Sharpeye

Those that insisted that I could/should not edit myself...>

OUTSIDE THE LINES

Published by Sharpeye - 2021

www.sharpeye.london